HEROES OF HISTORY

CAPTAIN JOHN SMITH

A Foothold in the New World

HEROES OF HISTORY

CAPTAIN JOHN SMITH

A Foothold in the New World

JANET & GEOFF BENGE

Emerald
Books

P.O. BOX 635, LYNNWOOD, WA 98046

Emerald Books are distributed through YWAM Publishing. For a full list of titles, including other great biographies, visit our website at www.ywampublishing.com or call 1-800-922-2143.

Captain John Smith: A Foothold in the New World
Copyright © 2006 by Janet and Geoff Benge

Published by Emerald Books
P.O. Box 635
Lynnwood, Washington 98046

Third printing 2016

Library of Congress Cataloging-in-Publication Data
Benge, Janet, 1958–
    John Smith : a foothold in the New World / Janet and Geoff Benge.
        p. cm. — (Heroes of history)
    Includes bibliographical references.
    ISBN-13: 978-1-932096-36-1 (pbk.)
    ISBN-10: 1-932096-36-1 (pbk.)
    1. Smith, John, 1580–1631—Juvenile literature. 2. Colonists—Virginia—Biography—Juvenile literature. 3. Explorers—America—Biography—Juvenile literature. 4. Explorers—Great Britain—Biography—Juvenile literature. 5. Jamestown (Va.)—History—17th century—Juvenile literature. 6. Jamestown (Va.)—Biography—Juvenile literature. 7. Virginia—History—Colonial period, ca. 1600–1775—Juvenile literature. I. Benge, Geoff, 1954– II. Title.
    F229.S7B46 2006
    973.21092—dc22   2006001862

Printed in the United States of America.

HEROES OF HISTORY
Biographies

Abraham Lincoln
Alan Shepard
Ben Carson
Benjamin Franklin
Billy Graham
Christopher Columbus
Clara Barton
Davy Crockett
Daniel Boone
Douglas MacArthur
Elizabeth Fry
George Washington
George Washington Carver
Harriet Tubman
John Adams
John Smith
Laura Ingalls Wilder
Louis Zamperini
Meriwether Lewis
Milton Hershey
Orville Wright
Ronald Reagan
Theodore Roosevelt
Thomas Edison
William Bradford
William Penn
William Wilberforce

Available in paperback, e-book, and audiobook formats.
Unit Study Curriculum Guides are available for each biography.
www.emeraldbooks.com

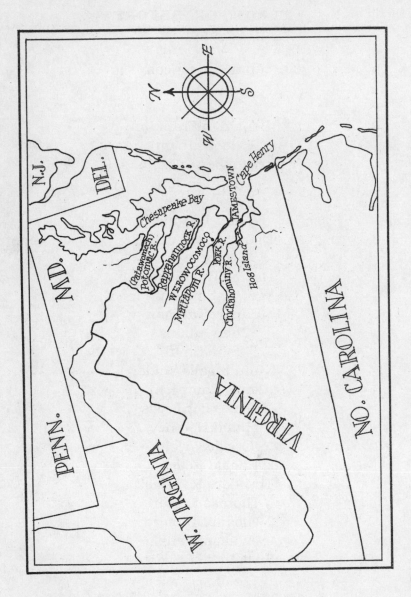

Contents

Chapter 1

Life in the Balance

John knew that he had to keep his wits about him at all costs. Sitting opposite him was a man clad in a raccoon-skin robe with a string of pearls around his neck. He was Chief Powhatan, whom no Englishman had ever set eyes on before. Women who surrounded the chief pointed at John and giggled.

One of the chief's daughters, about twelve years of age, whose name John learned was Amonute, sat staring at him and did not move her gaze as her father gave a long speech in Algonquian. John did not understand all of what the chief said, but he understood enough to realize that he was in deep trouble,

Finally Chief Powhatan raised his hand, and everything in the lodge fell silent except for the crackling of the logs in the fire in the middle of the room. The chief stared coldly and silently at John for a long time before he spoke. "You are one of the Englishmen. Why have you settled in our territory?" he asked. "And why have two of your ships left without you? When will they return?"

John thought quickly. He did not want to give the chief any information about the newly established English settlement or the colonists' long-term goals, lest Chief Powhatan decide to destroy the settlement. He concocted a story that would lead the chief to think that the camp was temporary and would soon be gone.

"As you are aware," John began, "there are three ships. These ships were involved in a fierce battle with England's enemy, the Spanish. They were damaged in the fight and were forced to seek shelter in Chesapeake Bay so that repairs could be made. The two ships you speak of have been repaired, but the third vessel is still leaking. The two ships have left for England to get supplies. When they return, we will finish repairing the other ship, and then we will all sail away together back to England."

John hoped that he sounded convincing, as Chief Powhatan held his life in the balance. But before he finished, he decided to raise the stakes on the chief. "I am a leader among the Englishmen, as you are among your people," John told Chief Powhatan. "My people expect me to return to the settlement soon. If I do not return, Englishmen will surely come looking for me. They will come carrying muskets and riding in boats armed with cannons."

Chief Powhatan sat in silence, contemplating what John had just said. Finally he gathered a group of his advisers to help him decide John's fate. John Smith could do nothing but await the verdict.

Finally Chief Powhatan made his decision. He signaled to several warriors standing at the door of the lodge. Moments later the men rolled in a large, flat stone and set it in front of the fire. Then two burly warriors emerged carrying heavy wooden clubs. John felt his pulse quicken. He knew that one of the means of execution the local Indians used was to place a man's head on a stone and smash his skull with heavy clubs. And that, apparently, was the end Chief Powhatan had chosen for John Smith.

Several warriors grabbed John and pulled him forward. They forced his head down onto the cold stone and stood back as the two warriors stepped forward and raised their clubs.

As John waited for the searing pain of the first blow against the side of his head, a million thoughts wanted to race through his mind. But the one that found voice was, *So this is how the life of the boy from Lincolnshire is going to end.*

Chapter 2

Dreams of Adventure

It was a warm summer morning in Lincolnshire in 1588, and eight-year-old John Smith and the two sons of Lord Willoughby, Peregrine and Robert Bertie, were making their way across the rolling green countryside to the ocean. They planned to build a boat when they reached their destination and sail away out into the North Sea. John's dream was to become just like Sir Francis Drake. Sir Francis was John's hero, not just because he was the first Englishman to sail around the world, but because just weeks before, Sir Francis had saved England from an invasion by the Spanish. In fact, the great regret in John's life was that his younger brother, and not he, had been given the name Francis.

As the boys walked along, they came upon the remains of a huge bonfire. John kicked at the ashes, sending a fine puff of cinders into the air. "You know what this is?" he asked.

Peregrine and Robert stared blankly at him.

"It's the remains of one of the signal fires warning of the approach of the Spanish armada," John said, answering his own question. "But we had a surprise for the Spanish. Sir Francis Drake was not about to let them invade England without a fight," he continued, using the opportunity to tell Peregrine and Robert all he knew about the incident. "Sir Francis and Sir John Hawkins made them pay. The English ships were faster and had better cannons than the Spanish. It wasn't long before ships of the armada were heading to the bottom of the sea at the hands of the English. And then a great storm blew up and sank many more of the Spanish ships. Soon what remained of the armada was retreating home to Spain, beaten once again by their old foe, Sir Francis Drake."

John puffed out his chest as he walked. When he grew up, he was going to be just like Sir Francis Drake. He was going to live a life full of adventure and conquest in far-flung corners of the earth. And when the boys reached the ocean, John's first adventure was going to begin.

At the beach John and the Bertie boys set to work building a raft. They located several logs washed up on the sand and dragged them to the water's edge. They lashed the logs together with the rope they had brought with them. Once they were satisfied that the logs were tied together tightly enough, they went in search of long sticks to pole the raft out to sea once it was launched.

By early afternoon they had found the sticks they needed, and the three boys began to drag the raft into the water. This was not easy work, but eventually, bit by bit, the boys nudged the logs forward until they were bobbing in the ocean. Once the raft was afloat, they pushed it out beyond the waves breaking at the shore and climbed aboard. John immediately took command of the vessel, standing at the back of the raft and shouting orders to Peregrine and Robert to pole harder.

So this is what it's like to be Sir Francis Drake, John thought as the raft left the shore behind and headed out into the North Sea. Now it was time to hunt for marauding Spanish ships and attack them.

"We're sinking! We're sinking!" came Peregrine's words, interrupting John's reverie.

Sure enough, when John brought his focus back to the raft, seawater was already washing over it.

"What are we going to do?" Robert fretted. "We can't swim!"

Suddenly John did not feel so brave. His adventure was quickly becoming a disaster. He scanned the sea around them for a boat or something floating on the surface that they could perhaps hold on to. That was when he saw the fishing boat approaching them, and he breathed a sigh of relief. "Look," he said, pointing toward the fishing boat.

When Peregrine and Robert saw the boat, they began waving their arms frantically to attract the attention of the fishermen aboard. By the time the fishing boat pulled alongside, the raft was completely swamped, and the boys were standing knee-deep in the water.

"Masters Bertie and Master Smith," the captain of the fishing boat said. "You seem to have gotten yourselves into a wee situation. Thought those water-logged logs would keep you afloat, did you?"

John nodded slightly, embarrassed by the observation.

"Well, you better come aboard quickly before that thing goes all the way to the bottom," the captain said.

The three boys clambered into the fishing boat, and soon they were sailing back toward the shore. When they reached dry land, two of the fishermen escorted the boys home and told Lord Willoughby and John's father what had happened.

John crept into the house. His mother was feeding baby Alice by the fireplace. Her eyebrows raised when she saw how wet John was, but she did not chastise him as he changed into dry clothes. Then, without having to be reminded, John picked up the milking pail and headed outside.

Soon John was sitting on the three-legged stool, listening to the rhythmic swishing of the milk against the side of the wooden pail. He wished he could stay there a long time, because he knew that once his chores were over, he was in for a lecture from his father. It would be the usual tirade in which George Smith asked his son why he could not be content to work on the farm or be grateful that one day he would be inheriting his own piece of land. That would be enough to make any other young boy in Lincolnshire happy. So why did John need to go off searching for adventures for himself?

It was a question John had no answer to. He knew his father was right—he should be grateful that one day he would inherit land. This in itself was enough to make the other boys living on Lord Willoughby's estate jealous. Their fathers, like John's, were tenant farmers on the estate, but unlike their fathers, John's father was also a land-holder, owning several orchards, a number of acres of pastureland, and at least two houses in the town of Louth that were rented out. The fact that he was a landowner as well as a tenant farmer gave George Smith a much higher social position. The Smiths were the only family on the estate who were regularly invited to the manor house to dine with Lord Willoughby and his family. And because of his father's position, John also got to attend school with the Bertie boys in the nearby town of Alford. At school he learned arithmetic, Latin, Greek, and English.

Despite the privileges, somehow deep inside John knew that he would not follow in his father's footsteps. He was different, different from his younger brother Francis, who did not even know whether Sir Francis Drake had headed east or west when he circumnavigated the world eight years before. And different from the Bertie boys, who were content to read about the new colonies being planted by Spain, France, and Portugal in the New World. John was not content to read about such things. He wanted to go to the New World for himself. And now that the English had conquered the Spanish armada and proved their superiority on the sea, he hoped that it would not be long before the English were also establishing settlements in the New World. His fear was that all the great adventures and discoveries in the world would be over before he was old enough to strike out on his own.

As John approached adulthood, he discovered that striking out on his own was not going to be as easy as he thought. When he was fifteen years old, opportunity knocked. Queen Elizabeth had just commissioned the formation of a new and permanent fleet, to be known as the Royal Navy, to protect English ships and coastline. This new navy was looking for recruits, and John was eager to apply. John's father, however, shut the door swiftly and firmly on this opportunity. Shortly after John's sixteenth birthday, he apprenticed John to a wealthy merchant, Thomas Sendall, in the nearby town of Lynn. Sendall had no children of his own, and he wanted to take on a promising young apprentice, with the hope of one day bringing him in as a partner in the company and possibly as an heir to his fortune.

Such an opportunity was wonderful for someone but not for John Smith. However, John did not have a say in the matter. As a result, he was packed up and sent off to live with his new master. John consoled himself with the hope that he might rise quickly to the position where he would be sent to France to buy silks or to Germany to find ironware.

John's hopes were soon dashed. John discovered that being a merchant's apprentice involved sitting at a table on a hard wooden stool, adding columns of figures and writing letters hour after hour. It was enough to make any young man's head hurt, especially in the winter months, when it was dark by four in the afternoon and he had to continue his work by candlelight.

The longer John sat at the desk, writing letters and adding figures, the less chance he could see of his getting out of the situation. The papers that apprenticed him to Thomas Sendall were legally binding documents. The only way out of them was to buy the papers. But this was impossible since John did not earn any money. In return for six years of labor, Sendall agreed to provide John with room and board but no other income and to instruct him in the ways of buying and selling.

Things were not made any easier when early in 1596 John learned that Sir Francis Drake had died and been buried at sea off the coast of Panama. With Sir Francis went John's hope of escaping his present situation and going off to serve with the world's most famous privateer. It was a bitter blow to John, and it made him feel more trapped than ever. Years of boredom loomed in front of him, until one day in the spring of 1596, his brother Francis burst into the store. Suddenly everything changed.

"It's Father. He just died!" Francis yelled frantically, even though he was standing right next to John. "Come on. Mother needs you."

John quickly obtained permission from Thomas Sendall to leave his desk, and then he jumped onto the back of Francis's horse. As the boys galloped through the Lincolnshire countryside, John tried to think about what his father's death would mean for him. He already knew that he was going to inherit seven acres of pastureland, three orchards, and most of his father's livestock, but how else would his life change? He supposed that his mother would expect him to buy his way out of his apprenticeship and return to the Willoughby estate to run the Smith family farm. But even before John arrived home to help prepare his father's body for burial, another plan was formulating in his mind. Yes, he would buy his way out of his apprenticeship, but not so that he could work on the farm. At sixteen years of age, he believed that it was time for him to see the world.

Chapter 3

Somewhere in Europe
an Adventure Awaited

B ut Mother, I may never get another opportunity like this!" John pleaded. "Just think of it. I won't be gone long, only six weeks. Robert will be with me the whole time. And when we get to France, Peregrine will be waiting for us. When the trip is over, I'll come home and return to my apprenticeship and help run the farm."

"Oh, John, I wish you wouldn't," Mrs. Smith sighed.

John bit his lip so that he would not break into a grin. He had won. Now that his mother had turned from forbidding him to go to France to wishing that he would not go, it was only a matter of time before she would give her consent. Sure enough, a week later, just three months after the death of his father, John was given permission to accompany Robert to

France to visit Robert's brother Peregrine, who was studying in Orléans.

Despite John's expectations, neither his mother nor Lord Willoughby, who was made executor of his father's estate, had agreed to John's buying his way out of his apprenticeship. Therefore John asked for and received permission from Thomas Sendall to take time off from his apprenticeship to make the trip to France. Before he set out, John sold some of the livestock he had inherited from his father. He gave half of the proceeds to his mother and kept the other half for his trip.

Soon everything was arranged and John and Robert were on their way to London to board a packet ship for the trip to France. They had promised Lord Willoughby that they would spend only one night in London, but once they saw the city, neither of them could tear himself away from it. There was so much to do and see. The young men wandered around Westminster Abbey, the biggest building either of them had ever seen, and then they went to view the Tower of London, where Queen Elizabeth had been imprisoned for two months by her sister Mary. They were also awed by St. James's Palace, which had been rebuilt fifty-five years before by King Henry VIII. John and Robert found that London had other things to offer as well. They gambled on fighting bears, drank beer at local taverns, and attended raucous performances of plays by a promising new playwright named William Shakespeare.

With all the things to see and do in London, it was a full week before John and Robert finally stepped aboard ship for the trip to France. In his childhood John had pretended hundreds of times to be aboard a sailing ship, but never once had he anticipated what happened to him once the ship slipped its moorings and sailed out of the mouth of the Thames River into the seething ocean. John became violently seasick and was forced to retreat below deck, where he swayed in a hammock, his stomach churning as the ship crossed the English Channel. Never once throughout the two-and-a-half-day voyage did he venture out on deck. He left his hammock only when the ship was finally at anchor in the harbor at St.-Valéry-sur-Somme on the north coast of France.

John was elated to be on land again, especially on foreign land. Robert arranged for them to hire horses, and soon the two young men were on their way to Paris to rendezvous with Peregrine. Paris was said to be the most sophisticated city in the world, and John could hardly wait to explore it.

Paris did not disappoint John, who had thought London was wonderful but found Paris to be magnificent. The city had more cobbled streets than any other city in Europe, and great marble statues adorned the streets and squares. The city also had a number of wonderful art galleries, the greatest being the Louvre, which was in the process of having a new wing added to it. And then there was the great cathedral of Notre Dame, whose size and architecture greatly impressed John. But Paris was more than just magnificent buildings. The city also had parks and more theaters than London did, and it seemed as though every corner had inns and restaurants that served the best food and wine John had ever tasted.

Paris offered so much to see and do that the six-week vacation flew by. As it drew to a close, John made a decision. He was not going to return home to Lincolnshire after all. Somewhere in Europe an adventure awaited him, and he intended to find it. Of course, by now John had run out of money and had to think of some way to get paid for his labor. He did not want to get stuck working in one place again, however, and neither was he eager to take to the sea after his bout with seasickness. One choice began to loom large in his mind—the French army.

Here's a chance to have it all: regular pay, companions along the way, and the opportunity to go farther afield than I've ever been before, John told himself. Besides, he liked what the French army was fighting for. King Henry IV of France was a Huguenot, or Protestant, king, and he was locked in a struggle with Catholic King Philip II of Spain over the future of France. Henry IV had a well-disciplined army, and in the ten years he had been fighting, he had slowly beaten back the Spanish and had unified France.

With high hopes John headed out into the hilly countryside near Le Havre where the French army was stationed. As he rode along on his horse, he thought about how to put himself in the best light to get hired by the army. He was only sixteen years old and had no experience at war, though he did cheer himself with the memory of fencing lessons with the Bertie boys. He was not the best horseman, but he could stay in the saddle, and he had been raised on a farm. And although he had never fired a gun or seen a cannon, he was sure that he would make a good marksman. The biggest mark against him was the fact that he spoke no French except for the few words he had picked up in Paris.

When John arrived at the French army camp, he spoke to a sergeant dressed in worn leather breeches and rusting armor. John did his best to explain to the sergeant that he wanted to join the army. The sergeant looked him up and down and then in French ordered him to leave camp. John, however, was determined to join the army, and he pretended not to understand the sergeant and continued to press his case. Again the gruff sergeant ordered him to leave, and again John stood his ground. But this time an English-speaking captain in the French army overheard the exchange. He called John over and explained that the French army was presently not accepting new recruits. He suggested that John try to join one of the mercenary companies that were fighting alongside the French army. "They are staying on the far side of the camp," he said, pointing John in their direction.

Although John had had his heart set on joining the French army, he accepted the captain's suggestion and made his way in the direction of the mercenary companies. After all, what choice did he have? He had used up all his money, and if he did not find a place in the army, he would be reduced to begging in the streets to survive.

On the far side of the army encampment, John came upon a mercenary company that consisted mostly of Englishmen. When he announced that he wanted to join the company, John was told that he would first have to pass a test. He would have to fight Luis de Toledo, the company's lieutenant and second in command. Luis was a grizzled man with a dark, weathered face that prominently featured his squished, broken nose. John's jaw dropped as Luis stripped to the waist, exposing a muscular, heavily scarred chest. John wanted to tell him to forget the whole idea, but he summoned his courage, stripped off his own shirt, and prepared for the fight.

John had been taught in school in England the importance of sportsmanship and playing by the rules. He soon learned that among mercenaries no such rules applied. No sooner had the fight begun than Luis gave John a swift kick to the groin. The pain was excruciating, and John felt his knees begin to buckle. In that instant his opponent lunged at him and wrestled him to the ground, biting his ear in the process. John collapsed to the ground, with Luis's bulky body on top of him. Immediately the lieutenant jumped back onto his feet and began a barrage of kicks and punches against John's body. John tried to struggle back onto his feet and fight back, but Luis was too much for him. The man's kicks and punches were doing their job, and the fight was over in a matter of minutes. Darkness enveloped John as he lapsed into unconsciousness.

When he finally regained consciousness, John was sure that he had failed the test. He was bloodied and bruised and had been beaten senseless in no time at all. But much to his surprise, John found Luis tending to his wounds, bathing them in cheap brandy.

"Congratulations, you have passed the test," the lieutenant said in broken English.

John could hardly believe it. He had made it into the ranks of the mercenaries.

John soon learned about the band of mercenaries he had joined. It was under the command of Captain Joseph Duxbury, the youngest son of an English baron who had squandered his inheritance gambling in London. Rather than face debtors' prison, Joseph had fled England and become a mercenary. While most of the members of the mercenary company were English, others were from Scotland, Ireland, and Germany, and there were even a few Spanish deserters like Luis de Toledo.

John also learned that a mercenary received no regular pay. Mercenaries made their money by looting traitors' homes and stripping dead bodies in battle. But since a battle had not taken place for several months, the mercenary troops had had no income. Each morning Captain Duxbury provided a piece of meat and a loaf of bread, which the men could eat throughout the day. John was given a plumed steel helmet, which constituted the company's uniform. John soon learned that, apart from that, he was on his own. Since no blankets were issued to the men, John spent a cold, sleepless first night with his new company. The other mercenaries laughed and told him he would not be warm until they had fought someone and pillaged blankets and fresh clothes.

The idea of fighting worried John. No training was going on in the camp, and since John had no horse and no weapon, it did not seem likely that he would be much help in a battle. In fact, he suspected that he would probably be killed within minutes in such an action. Eventually Captain Duxbury did give John an old musket to use as a weapon, but the gun disappeared one night while John was sleeping.

One day dragged on after another. The men usually gambled away the morning and then drank away the afternoon and night in the local public houses. But participation in such activities required money, and John did not have a penny to his name. Eventually boredom led him to walk to nearby villages, and in one such village, called Harfleur, he noticed a help-wanted sign on the door of a butcher's shop.

John learned that the butcher's two sons were away in the army and that the man desperately needed someone to help him cut up beef, mutton, and ox meat in the afternoons. The butcher explained to John that he could not offer him very much money, but in exchange for his labor he could pay him a small amount and give him a hearty dinner cooked by his wife each day and a jug of beer with his dinner. Since he had nothing else to do, John took the job and soon found himself elbow-deep in animal carcasses. He did not mind the work. He had helped his father butcher sheep and cows back on the farm when he was growing up. Sometimes as he worked, John wondered whether he was ever going to have a great adventure. Or had he simply replaced one form of boredom for another?

Then one hot summer's day John's mercenary company, along with the other seven mercenary companies stationed around Le Havre, was on the march. The men's orders were to find Spanish troops in northern France and kill them. John was glad to be moving. At least he was on the first day. By the second day, his feet were raw with blisters and he was tired of marching behind horses that seemed to do nothing but kick up the dust.

Eleven days after they set out, the troops were still marching. Then, on the twelfth day, Captain Duxbury reported that Spanish troops were encamped nearby at Grandvilliers. The news invigorated the mercenaries, who, upon learning that the Spanish had retreated into the walled city and closed the gates, knew that it was time for action.

The mercenaries headed for the manor house where the Spanish had been staying. John complained to himself as he marched along that the men on horseback would get there long before he did and would have first pickings of the loot at the house. However, when he finally arrived on the scene, John realized that he was in luck. His comrades were swarming through the house, grabbing what they could, but no one had touched the barn.

John nudged a fellow mercenary who was also on foot, and together the two of them crept away and made a dash for the barn. Once there, John discovered that several horses had been left behind. He raced to a stall and claimed one of the animals for himself, a four-year-old bay gelding. He also grabbed a saddle for his new mount and a thick, woolen cloak. And to his surprise, he found an old sword propped in the corner of the stall that housed his new horse. In less than fifteen minutes, John had claimed his horse, saddled the animal, and led it outside, where he mounted it.

Sitting proudly on his new horse, John felt like part of everything. He had a horse, a saddle, a cloak, and a useful weapon. He held his head high as he rode along. He was a gentleman soldier now, ready and equipped for a real battle.

Chapter 4

Something of a Legend

John laughed at the story his fellow mercenary told him. Thank goodness, he told himself, that his three companions on patrol were the lively story-tellers of the company, as the stories helped pass the time. The four of them were patrolling a narrow strip of land three hundred yards along the outside of the wall of the French city of Amiens. They had been walking their horses back and forth along the same short stretch for three days now. It was not a glamorous assignment, but it was a necessary one. Just two weeks before, on March 18, 1597, the Spanish army had broken through French lines and captured the city of Amiens. This provoked King Henry IV to move quickly. Amiens was the gateway to the French lowlands, and if the Spanish kept their foothold there and pushed on, they could soon overrun France completely.

John admired the way the French king had taken control of the troops as they held Amiens under siege. No one would be permitted to leave or enter the city until it had eventually run out of food and water and the Spanish troops holed up there had surrendered. Outfitted with muskets and pistols, John and his three companions were assigned to patrol one small section of the wall so that no one could sneak in or out of the city. The path that the horses trod as the men patrolled the area skirted a ravine with deep, wooded sides and boulders strewn about.

The task was, for the most part, a boring one. The men had to be in the saddle patrolling for eighteen hours each day, and they were not permitted to dismount their horses to eat or drink. At the end of the eighteen hours another group of mercenaries was sent to relieve them so that they could return to camp and eat and sleep for six hours. Still, John hoped that it would not be all boredom, that eventually he would see some real action, especially as the siege dragged on and those trapped inside became desperate.

As it happened, John did not have to wait too long to get his wish. He and his three companions had just reached the southern end of the three-hundred-yard strip they patrolled and were turning their horses to head north again when John saw them. A platoon of Spanish soldiers had somehow sneaked out of Amiens and was charging toward them on horseback. John's mind raced. With the ravine behind and beside them, the four mercenaries were trapped. They had to do something or they would be slaughtered, though John doubted that they would survive even if they did take action. Still, they had to try.

"This way. Follow me," John barked at his three companions.

With that, John spurred his horse to a full gallop and headed straight at the platoon of Spanish soldiers. The other three men fell in behind him, their horses also at full gallop.

Without slowing down, John grabbed the musket slung over his left shoulder. As best he could, he raised the musket, aimed, and fired it. The bullet from his gun smashed into the shoulder of the Spanish lieutenant leading the charge. As the lieutenant slumped over in the saddle, his horse veered to the right and galloped away.

Despite the injury to their commanding officer, the remainder of the Spanish platoon kept charging forward. John kept charging too. Since he did not have time to reload his musket, he pulled a pistol from his belt. Again he took aim as best he could and fired. This time, though, instead of hitting one of the soldiers, he hit one of their horses. The animal toppled to the ground, sending its rider skidding across the ground.

By now John's three fellow mercenaries had their muskets raised, and they fired off a volley. Their bullets found the mark, injuring two of the Spanish soldiers and killing another one. Suddenly the horses carrying the Spanish soldiers began to slow and scatter. The men were giving up the fight. They turned their horses and began to gallop away as the four mercenaries quickly reloaded their muskets and fired after them.

"That was a very brave thing to do, if a little foolhardy," one of John's fellow mercenaries admonished him after the Spanish soldiers had fled back into Amiens. "You're a braver man than I. I did not see any way that we could get out of that fix alive."

The story of John's heroic and foolhardy exploit was retold by his comrades so many times around the campfire that John became something of a legend among the men, so much so that Captain Duxbury promoted him to the rank of sergeant. His bravery also brought John to the attention of the king of France, and that pleased John more than anything else.

King Henry IV quickly became John's hero. He was a highly intelligent man who chose to lead his men into battle rather than order them out in front of him. Moreover, he often went on all-night patrols with the troops and took his turn doing duties with all of the soldiers. And now that John had distinguished himself, King Henry often rode on patrols with him, explaining his plan to win the siege against the Spanish. But despite the king's plans, the siege dragged on and on through a wet spring and then a sweltering hot summer. Somehow the French people and Spanish soldiers trapped within the walls of Amiens were managing to survive. The Spanish were even able to keep up regular volleys of musket shots and arrows aimed against those outside the wall besieging the city.

At midsummer the Spanish were able to fool one of the French generals, allowing them to slip in supplies to replenish the beleaguered city. Since King Henry IV worried that the siege might drag on indefinitely if he did not take some decisive action, he called for more troops from Paris. It was time to mount an all-out assault against Amiens, something John had been hoping for weeks would happen.

Alas, John's hopes were dashed. When King Philip II of Spain learned of the upcoming attack against Amiens, he decided that it was time to surrender, which he did on September 25, 1597. The war between France and Spain came to an end. This was a double disappointment for John. Not only was there no battle, but also the mercenaries were not allowed to plunder the city, since it was now back in French hands. However, with the war over, King Henry generously paid off the mercenaries who had fought for France.

With nothing more than his pay in hand, John set out on his next adventure. He had gained a taste for the soldier's life, and when Captain Duxbury announced that he was leading a march to Amsterdam, Holland, to keep King Philip II of Spain from retaking that country, John was the first to sign up. He was only seventeen years old, but as the march began, he was already a war hero who had seen more of the world than many men twice his age.

The march northeast to Holland was a comfortable one. The mercenaries who had signed up to go and fight had plenty of money in their pockets and strong horses to ride. Occasionally John wondered what was going on back home in Lincolnshire, but he never felt a longing to return there. Seeing Europe and fighting wars was far too much fun to swap for the life of an English farmer.

Fortunately for Holland, King Philip II died suddenly on September 13, 1598, and it took the Spanish a little over a year to regroup. In that time they did not gain an inch of Dutch territory. Then, in early 1600, the new king, Philip III, was ready to press on with the conquest of Holland. He ordered a series of assaults against the country, which John and his mercenary band helped repel. Then on July 1, 1600, the Dutch took the offensive and attacked a Spanish stronghold at Nieuport, in neighboring Belgium. As usual John was at the forefront of the action.

The Spanish could have indefinitely withstood the assault against their fortified position at Nieuport, since it was located on the coast and could be easily resupplied from the sea. But Maurice of Nassau, president of the Dutch Council of State and commander in chief of the country's army, was a brilliant military tactician, and he devised a plan to lure the Spanish out of their fortifications. He had a small force attack Nieuport directly. The Spanish took his bait. Thinking that this was the best force the Dutch could muster, they opened the gates to the city and sent out several regiments of soldiers to destroy their enemy. However, once these Spanish soldiers left the safety of the walled city, several companies of mercenaries, including John's, charged in behind the Spanish troops, cutting off their route of escape back into Nieuport. Seeing the predicament of their troops, the Spanish were forced to send out the remaining troops in the city as reinforcements. But no sooner had these soldiers left their fortifications than Dutch troops stormed in behind them and also cut off their route of escape. With his troops in place, Maurice gave the order to attack.

Captain Duxbury's company of mercenaries were in the middle of the cavalry line that now charged forward to attack the Spanish troops. John didn't even seem to notice the musket balls and arrows that burst around him. With his feet planted firmly in the stirrups and his sword in hand, he stood and encouraged the other mercenaries forward. At the same time he swung his sword from side to side, striking down and killing as many Spanish soldiers as he could.

The ferocious battle lasted for less than an hour, and when it was over, Maurice of Nassau and his army had won a stunning victory over the superior Spanish troops.

When the battle ended, many of the Spanish troops fled in retreat, with the mercenaries right behind to hunt down and kill as many of them as they could. As John galloped along after a Spanish officer, the officer managed to turn and fire off a bullet from his revolver. The bullet hit John, causing him to fall from his horse, and John had to be carried from the battlefield by his comrades.

John was too badly injured to return to Holland with the rest of his company. Instead he was boarded in the home of a Nieuport merchant, who promised to see that he was nursed back to health. Six weeks passed before John had recovered enough to begin the journey back to Holland. Captain Duxbury had taken John's horse with him, and so John had no choice but to walk the entire way to Holland. He made slow progress, but he was well rewarded when he was finally reunited with his men. The men gave him a rousing welcome, and Captain Duxbury promoted him once again, this time to the rank of ensign. This made John third in command of the company, quite an honor for such a young man.

Another honor also awaited John.

"Here, you must read this, John," Captain Duxbury said soon after John's return. He handed John a copy of Maurice of Nassau's report on the battle at Nieuport and pointed to one particular paragraph. John began to read:

> The paid horsemen rode in the van, and were inspired by the example of an English sergeant in the Duxbury company, one Jon Smyt [Smith], who laid about him with such rapid strokes that he left a path of Spanish dead in his wake. Other horsemen pressed close with matching fervor, and soon the paid listors [mercenary companies] reached the enemy rear. Whilst they turned and made ready to ride again. From rear to front, our valiant regiments were upon the foe, who scattered in disarray.

"Other than the regimental commanders of the Dutch army, you are the only other individual to be mentioned by name in the report," Captain Duxbury said, giving John a congratulatory clap on the shoulder. John felt his chest puff out in pride at his accomplishment.

John had no further opportunity, however, to use his new rank. Following their defeat, the Spanish had begun negotiating a peace agreement with the Dutch, and the mercenary companies were disbanded. Many of the members of the mercenary companies decided to journey on to Austria to fight an onslaught of Muslim Turks. John thought long and hard about joining them, but in the end he decided it was time to go home and check up on his family. He had left England for a six-week holiday, and now he had been gone for four years. Still, since he was in no particular hurry to get to Lincolnshire, he decided to spend a few weeks in Amsterdam, taking in the sights of the city with Captain Duxbury.

After Captain Duxbury and John had wandered up and down and around the narrow streets of Amsterdam and taken a number of boat rides along the canals that divided the city, Captain Duxbury introduced John to a middle-aged man named Peter Plancius. Peter was Holland's foremost geographer, and John was instantly fascinated by his knowledge of maps and exploration. For the next several weeks, John spent most of his time at Peter's house, where he was shown the most recent maps of the New World. Together the two men speculated about what might lie beyond the boundaries of the known world.

When it was finally time for John to return to England, he was sad to leave his new friend behind. He did not go away empty-handed, however. In Latin, Peter had written a letter of introduction for John to Richard Hakluyt, his counterpart and colleague in London.

The letter of introduction in hand, John boarded an English merchant ship bound for London. Being the only passenger aboard, John ate with the crew and helped square the rigging. He also found that he was not troubled in the same way by seasickness as he had been on the journey to France. As the journey progressed, John discovered that the captain of the ship, Henry Hudson, was an extraordinary man who proved to be a master mariner. When a vicious storm blew up, Henry seemed to know its mood and where exactly to maneuver his ship so that it did not bear the full brunt of the wind and waves. John also learned that Henry had sailed with Captain John Davis on a voyage of discovery that took them to Greenland and along the northeastern coast of the American continent. Henry was full of stories of this adventure, and he and John would sit late into the night talking.

In fact, John was rather astonished by the events of the past few weeks. He had just come from spending time with one of the most knowledgeable geographers in all Europe, and now he was listening to tales from a widely traveled master mariner. Only time would tell how these two events would propel John into his own place in history.

Chapter 5

Captain John Smith

When the ship from Holland finally arrived in London, Henry invited John to stay with him, his wife, and his four children for a week. John accepted the invitation, and soon he and Henry were busy discussing exploring the unknown world. Henry explained to John his idea of there being an unobstructed passage to the East Indies. "Such a passage must be either by way of the North Pole or across the great continent of North America," Henry said.

While in London, John visited Richard Hakluyt at Westminster. He handed Richard the letter of introduction that Peter Plancius had written, and the two men became instant friends. Richard proved to be just as interesting and knowledgeable of the world as Peter was.

After a week in London, John said good-bye to his new friends and headed north to Lincolnshire. He decided to arrive home in style, riding a new, dappled horse and wearing a fashionable silver helmet. His saddlebags were full of silver and gifts for his own family and the family of Lord Willoughby.

John soon learned that much had happened during the time he was away. His brother Francis had married and settled down into the life of a farmer. Meanwhile, a farmer was courting his sister Alice, and when John asked questions about him, Alice became very upset. John soon realized that although he was her big brother, he had been away a long time, and now that he was back, no one wanted him to take up his old position in the family. John's mother was doing well, but Lord Willoughby had died the year before. Now Peregrine Bertie was the new Lord Willoughby. John visited him and found that he too was caught up in the everyday affairs of his small realm, though he was eager to hear all about John's adventures on the European continent.

As it turned out, so many people came to listen to John recount his tales of adventure that he soon grew weary of all the attention. He asked the new Lord Willoughby if he could build himself a small lean-to deep in the forest and live there off the birds and deer that inhabited the place, supplementing his diet with dried goods that he would take with him. Peregrine gave his permission, and John soon retired to his camp in the forest to think and recover from the strain of war. He did not even take a change of clothes with him, though he did allow himself one luxury—books.

While he was away in Europe, John had learned something very important about himself. He realized that even though he had not gone on to university to study, he was an intelligent man who learned languages easily. Now he wanted to stretch his mind as far as it would go. He borrowed books from the manor house and from a friend who lived several miles away. The books included those by his new friend Richard Hakluyt; a collection of maps drawn by Peter Plancius; a philosophy book by Marcus Aurelius, a second-century Roman emperor, titled *Meditations*; and another volume, *The Arte of Warre,* by an Italian named Machiavelli. The latter book explained in detail how to acquire, maintain, and use military force against various enemies. Since *The Arte of Warre* was written in Italian, John took a bilingual dictionary with him so that he could teach himself how to read it. John also studied religion during this time, hoping to find some sense in the fighting between Catholics and Protestants in Europe.

Each day John had nothing to do except read and study, draw water, light a fire, and hunt for food. He emerged from his forest hideout once a week to visit his mother and collect a new supply of tapered tallow candles that she had made for him.

Six months later John left his forest campsite rested and with a new plan. He now knew for sure that he would never be content farming in England, nor did he care to go and fight Catholics again. The whole idea of Christians killing each other disgusted him. Instead he settled on a new cause. This time he would travel to the far reaches of Eastern Europe and help the Austrians and Hungarians repulse the Muslim Turks who had occupied large areas of their territory.

This was not a popular decision with John's mother, who begged her son to settle down. In response John made one concession. He agreed to leave his money with his brother Francis rather than take it with him. In this way, his mother argued, if he did return safely, he would have something to live on.

On the last day of July 1601, John set sail for France. He wore light armor and his silver helmet and armed himself with a sword, pistol, and double-edged knife, which he kept in the top of his boot. Whatever lay ahead, he felt ready to take it on.

The first leg of his voyage across the English Channel to France was uneventful. As on his voyage back from Holland with Henry Hudson, John found that he was no longer afflicted with seasickness. Once in France, John made his way overland to Marseilles, on the south coast, where he boarded another ship bound for Italy.

This next leg of his journey turned out to be hair-raising. From the moment he climbed the gangplank to board the vessel, John felt ill at ease. The other passengers aboard were all Catholics, from various countries, making a pilgrimage to Rome. John did his best not to stand out, but it was obvious that he was an Englishman and a Protestant.

Things went from bad to worse on the second day of the voyage. The ship encountered a severe storm, and huge waves tossed the vessel around. By evening many of the passengers were on their knees praying for their lives. As it turned out, no one needed to pray harder than John Smith, because the other passengers suddenly turned on him.

"All Englishmen are pirates," one passenger yelled.

"And Protestants! God has sent this storm because of you!" another screamed at John above the howl of the wind.

The mainsail cracked above them in the ferocious wind as a group of red-faced men descended on John.

"You have brought a curse on us. Overboard with you," one of the men yelled.

A chorus of cheers went up. It was the last sound John heard before he was unceremoniously dumped over the side of the ship.

The dark, roiling sea engulfed John. He struggled to get to the surface, but he was not even sure which way was up or down. Eventually, though, his head burst through the surface just in time. He gasped for breath and gulped in air before being pulled back under again. As he went down, he caught in the glare of a flash of lightning a glimpse of the ship bobbing over the next wave.

It was all John could do to stay afloat until the storm finally began to calm and he was able to make out the outline of an island in the moonlight. The ship had disappeared into the darkness, along with his money, armor, and weapons. But he could not think about that now. He had to concentrate on getting to the island.

Slowly, fighting every inch of the way, John splashed his way toward the beach. By the time he finally got there, he was too exhausted to even pull himself completely out of the water. He lay facedown on the sand, panting for breath.

When the sun came up, John staggered to his feet. He walked along the beach for about a mile and saw no sign of human life or habitation. Then, when he rounded a point, he saw a ship at anchor. The vessel had obviously taken shelter from the storm in a small cove. John frantically waved his hands to signal the ship, and eventually a small boat was lowered over the side and rowed ashore to pick him up.

John soon learned that the ship was a privateer commanded and crewed by a group of Bretons, from Brittany in France. John poured out his tale of woe to the captain about how he had come to be marooned on the island. As he talked, John noticed that the captain was beginning to warm to him. Sure enough, it was not long before the captain had outfitted John in a set of dry clothes and armed him with a sword and pistol. The captain also invited John to join the crew of his privateer. John agreed, since the alternative was being marooned. For the next six months he sailed all over the Mediterranean Sea, visiting Cyprus, Greece, and Alexandria in Egypt, places he never dreamed he would ever see. Along the way the men on the ship attacked and plundered a number of smaller ships. During his time aboard the privateer, John learned a lot about sailing and seamanship.

Finally, after six months, John disembarked in Naples, Italy. He left the ship a lot richer than when he had come aboard. As he walked down the gang-plank onto the dock in Naples, John had 225 pounds in his coat pocket, his share of the loot the privateer's crew had plundered from other ships during the six months John was aboard. This was a lot of money, more than enough to enjoy the sights, sounds, and food of Italy, as well as to buy himself a new set of armor and a horse.

After stopping for a while in Rome, John made his way north through Italy to Austria, where he finally met up with Archduke Ferdinand's army, which was fighting the Turks. Things went well for John from the start. John felt very much at home among the many different cultures represented in his unit. As well as coming from England, the other men had come from Scotland, Holland, Italy, Wales, and France. With his language skills, John was able to communicate with more of the men than anybody else in the company. This soon brought John to the attention of his commander, the Earl of Meldritch, who asked John whether he had any ideas on how to relieve the Hungarian town of Oberlimbach, which had been surrounded and was now under siege by twenty thousand Turks. Trapped inside the besieged town was a contingent of Austrian soldiers under the command of a man named Ebersbaught.

Oddly enough, John knew this man Ebersbaught. The two men had met when John first joined the army. During his time of reading and study in the forest back in Lincolnshire, John had learned of a technique of using three torches to send signals on the battlefield, and for some reason he had told Ebersbaught about it. He recalled the conversation they'd had.

"Do you have any special military skills?" Ebersbaught had asked him.

"I know a way to send secret messages without having to send a messenger who might get caught by the enemy," John replied.

Ebersbaught's eyebrows had raised at this. "Tell me more about this method," he said.

John had explained to Ebersbaught how by using one torch you could communicate the first letters of the alphabet. By showing a single light once, you signal the letter A, by showing a single light twice, you signal B, and a single light shown three times was C. This worked until you reached the letter M. When you wanted to signal the letter M, you used two torches. Showing two lights once was M, and two lights twice was N, and so on until you came to Z.

"But how does the person receiving the message know when a word ends?" Ebersbaught had asked.

"For that the sender holds up three torches at once. And since light can go anywhere, you do not need to send a messenger. Neither can the enemy stop the message," John said.

"It is a very clever way to send messages. Here, write the code down for me," Ebersbaught said.

Now John wondered whether Ebersbaught still had a copy of the code with him. He had a hunch that he might, and if he did, John had a plan of action.

The plan involved using exploding fireworks at night to trick the Turks into thinking they were under attack by a large contingent of troops. When the Turks diverted their attention to repel the attack, the Austrian army under the Earl of Meldritch's command would charge in from the side and catch the Turks off guard. At the same time, Ebersbaught and his contingent of soldiers would break out of the town and attack the Turks from the rear. Ebersbaught would know when to do this because John would send him a coded message using three torches.

It took a little while, but eventually John convinced the Earl of Meldritch that the plan would work. On Thursday night John crept up to the top of a rise opposite the besieged town of Oberlimbach. There he lit three torches and began sending a message to Ebersbaught inside the city. He spelled out the plan letter by letter, word by word, and then waited. Sure enough, within a few minutes three torches blazed from on top of the city wall, and Ebersbaught confirmed that he understood the message. John's plan was working.

The next day the troops busily prepared hundreds of exploding fireworks that would mimic the sight and sound of muskets being fired. After darkness had fallen, John and several comrades crept out into the blackness and set up the fireworks. At the appointed time, midnight, the fireworks were set off.

The plan worked perfectly. The Turks were fooled into thinking they were under attack, and as they diverted their attention to repel the charge, the Austrian troops rushed in from the side and Ebersbaught's army attacked from the rear. The unsuspecting Turks were caught in a trap and routed, and the town of Oberlimbach was liberated.

John's commanding officer was so impressed by the result that he promoted him, giving him command over a unit containing 250 men on horseback. And since John had done so well coming up with a plan to liberate Oberlimbach, the Earl of Meldritch turned over another problem to him, a much more longstanding problem—the city of Alba Regalis.

Alba Regalis was located closer to the Hungarian heartland in Transdanubia, and for sixty years the Turks had held the city. Thirty thousand Hungarian fighters were besieging the city, but the place was thought to be impregnable, even with a force twice that size.

Once again John came up with a plan. He oversaw his men as they filled large earthen pots with gunpowder. The pots were then covered in pitch laced with sulfur and turpentine. Quartered musket balls were then embedded in the pitch, and the pots were then wrapped in canvas. Finally a wick soaked in linseed oil, camphor, and sulfur was inserted into each pot. The men prepared fifty such pots, which John called his "fiery dragons."

Large catapults were maneuvered into place and aimed at the section of Alba Regalis where the Turks were known to gather, especially when under attack. At midnight the barrage began. The wicks of the fiery dragons were lit, and they were catapulted over the city wall. In the city they exploded, setting fire to the surrounding buildings and sending a hail of quartered musket balls in all directions.

The fiery dragons did their job well, decimating the Turkish soldiers inside the city so completely that when the thirty thousand Hungarian fighters charged the city, they met little resistance from the Turks and quickly overran the place. After sixty years, Alba Regalis had finally been wrested from enemy hands.

Once again John was the hero of the moment, and soon his name and exploits were legend throughout the Austrian and Hungarian armies.

John's next big challenge came at the Transylvanian town of Orastie, which the Turks were also holding. Hungarian forces were besieging the town, slowly digging trenches around it and positioning their catapults and other pieces of artillery. For whatever reason, the Turks seemed to become bored by all these preparations and proposed a duel between an officer in the Hungarian army and a Turkish nobleman named Turbashaw. John volunteered for the assignment. The two men agreed that they would be mounted on horseback and would carry lances and swords as weapons.

At the appointed time, Turbashaw emerged from behind the fortified wall of Orastie with great fanfare, a parade of servants bearing his armor and weapons. When Turbashaw had finally put on his armor and mounted his horse, John rode out from behind army lines, his lance tucked under one arm and his helmet under the other. The two combatants rode up to each other and bowed. They then rode on seventy-five paces in opposite directions.

John put on his helmet, tightened the straps on the side of his armor, wrapped his arm around his lance, and held up the lance, ready to charge. When a pistol sounded, he dug his heels into the side of his horse and the animal broke into an immediate gallop.

As John and Turbashaw raced at each other, John saw the weakness in his opponent's armor—a small gap between the top of Turbashaw's breastplate and his helmet. John stretched out his arm and aimed his lance at the gap. As the two horses swooped by each other, John's lance found its mark, sending Turbashaw hurtling backwards off his horse to the ground. By the time John had dismounted and walked over to his opponent, Turbashaw was dead.

One of Turbashaw's friends, a man named Grualgo, was incensed that John had killed his friend, and he immediately challenged John to a duel the next day. John accepted, and the following afternoon he once again rode out to do battle.

This time the men had agreed to arm themselves with lances, swords, and pistols. Once again John galloped at his opponent with his lance out, but this time he was unable to penetrate Grualgo's armor or dislodge him from his horse. The two combatants reeled their horses for another charge. By the time John had turned his horse and gotten it up again to a gallop, Grualgo had discarded his lance and drawn his pistol. He fired at John, who jerked his horse to the left. The bullet from the pistol hit John's armor with a glancing blow, denting it, but not injuring John.

Now it was John's turn. He grabbed his pistol, aimed it, and fired. The bullet penetrated Grualgo's shoulder right where his breastplate and the armor on his arm came together. Grualgo fell to the ground from his horse, injured. In an instant John was standing beside him. He drew his sword and struck Grualgo before he could fight back. Once again John rode back victorious.

Two days later it was John who issued a challenge to the Turks to send out their best officer to fight him. A man by the name of Buenimolgri, or Bonny Mulgro, as John called him, accepted the challenge. This time the men agreed to fight with battle-axes, pistols, and swords.

As the two men galloped toward each other, they drew their pistols and fired. Each man missed the other. They turned their horses and charged again, this time using their battle-axes. Back and forth the two went, combating each other with their vicious battle-axes. They managed to dent each other's armor, but neither man had the advantage, that is, until Bonny Mulgro managed to strike John on the side of his helmet with his battle-axe. The force of the blow sent John sideways. His foot slipped out of the stirrup, but he did not fall completely from his horse.

While John struggled to get his balance back and right himself in the saddle, Bonny Mulgro moved in for the kill. A huge cheer went up from the

Turks watching the duel from the walls of Orastie. As Bonny Mulgro raised his battle-axe to deliver a final blow, John saw the man's weak point: a small gap in his armor. In a single move, while still off balance, John grabbed the handle of his sword, pulled it from its scabbard, and struck his opponent at his weak point. Bonny Mulgro crumpled off his horse to the ground.

It was a great victory for John, one that left the Turks deflated. Soon afterward Orastie fell to the Christian troops besieging it.

Prince Zsigmond of Transylvania was so amazed at John's bravery in the fight with the Turks that he rewarded him with an insignia bearing the head of three Turks and awarded him an annual pension of three hundred ducats. In addition, John's commanding officer promoted him to the rank of captain and gave him a fresh horse and sword and a belt worth three hundred ducats.

Captain John Smith was elated. He had fought hard and won, but as he was accepting the cheers and rewards of his comrades, he had no idea how quickly victory could turn to ashes.

Chapter 6

Enslaved

I believe we are in deep trouble, Captain Smith," the Earl of Meldritch said, turning in his saddle to face John. "I've let us get too far ahead of the rest of the army, and I think we have marched into a trap."

John looked up at the high Transylvanian Alps that loomed to the east and to the west. The 35,000-man Austrian army was several days march behind the Earl of Meldritch's advance corps of three thousand troops as they trudged up the Oltu River valley, climbing toward the high pass that led over the mountains ahead of them.

"What makes you think it's a trap?" John asked, fingering his revolver.

"I've been watching the hills above us, and every so often I think I see movement and flashes of light.

My guess is that there are Turks up there watching our every move," the Earl of Meldritch replied.

John looked up at the snow-covered mountains, which had plenty of room to hide an army among the crevices and scrubby trees. Just then some rocks came cascading down the mountainside, and John caught a glimpse of a man waving to someone farther down the valley. He felt his pulse quicken.

"You're right," John said. "I just saw a signaler. We must assume the worst and act fast if we're to save ourselves."

The Earl of Meldritch nodded. "We're hemmed in here, and a cunning commander would have Turkish troops marching to attack our rear as well as our vanguard. That way we would be trapped with nowhere to go. Captain Smith, you and your men hold our forward position while I have the rest of the men chop down pine trees and stake them into the ground to form a palisade. Let's hope that will stop the Turkish cavalry from swooping in and destroying us and will give us a fighting chance to get out of this situation."

John ordered his men to follow as he galloped off toward the vanguard, casting a wary eye upwards as he did so. A hundred Turks situated on the high ground that surrounded the valley would easily have the advantage over a thousand fighting men on the floor of the valley.

John and his corps of 250 horsemen took up position. Several times they had to charge at advancing Turkish soldiers, fending them off while the rest of the Earl of Meldritch's men hastily built a square

palisade behind which they could take cover and
fight.

Finally the palisade was complete, and John and
his men fell back behind it. Although the evenly
spaced pine logs staked into the ground would pre-
vent the Turkish cavalry troops from galloping in
with their scimitars drawn, they also prevented the
Earl of Meldritch's cavalry from operating as it normally did in battle. As a result, John and his men
were forced to dismount and fight like infantrymen.

John's men had just enough time to dismount
and take up position before the first wave of Turkish
cavalry charged at them. But the stakes of the palisade slowed their advance enough for the Earl of
Meldritch's musketeers and archers to fire off volley
after volley. The men's bullets and arrows found their
mark, and the Turks were forced to retreat. They
withdrew only long enough to re-form their lines
and charge once more. Again the musketeers and
archers opened fire and beat the enemy back. But
again the Turkish cavalry regrouped and charged,
with the same result. And then they attacked a
fourth time.

By now the Turks were attacking the flanks of
the Earl of Meldritch's army. The Austrian soldiers
were under pressure from all sides, and by late
afternoon they had exhausted their supply of gunpowder and arrows. Turkish foot soldiers now
rushed forward unchecked and pulled down the
stakes that formed the palisade. Then their cavalry
charged in, the scimitars they wielded above their
heads glistening in the golden rays of the setting

sun. The rout was on, and John knew that they had no way to stop it. Still he determined to fight valiantly until the end and to kill as many Turkish soldiers as he could in the process.

John watched in horror as a number of the men tried to swim across the Oltu River to the high ground on the other side and make a stand against the Turks from there. But their heavy armor dragged them to the bottom of the river, where they drowned.

By the time darkness finally enveloped the battlefield, the battle was over. Most of the Earl of Meldritch's men lay dead or wounded. John Smith was lying in a pool of blood, having been knocked unconscious during the battle by a heavy sword blow to his helmet. He came to with a lantern shining in his eyes and his head throbbing. He heard someone yell in Turkish and then felt a rough kick to his side. As John recoiled in pain, two pairs of hands reached down and pulled him to his feet. The men stripped off his silver officer's armor and then removed his underclothes until he stood naked. They then poked at the wound in his arm and talked privately to each other.

John could tell from the tone of the men's voices that they were arguing about something. He prayed that it was not whether or not to kill him. The next thing John knew, he was being dragged through the corpses to a forge that had been set up at the entrance to the valley.

Evidently the Turks had been sure of victory, because hundreds of iron bands were sitting beside the forge. One of the bands was placed around

John's neck, and then a red-hot iron rivet from the forge was used to snap it closed. John could feel searing heat from the rivet as it was placed through the two holes in the flange of the ring and its end then hammered flat, locking the ring in place. He was now a prisoner with an iron ring around his neck. John, still naked, was then chained up to other prisoners and led over to a grassy plain, where a Turkish soldier motioned for them to lie down and rest.

Men groaned as they sank to the ground in the darkness. John could hear cries of pain and even sobbing, but he did not make a sound. He assumed that they had a long march ahead of them as prisoners, and anyone who did not look fit enough to march would most likely be killed in the morning. John's number-one objective became getting out of the valley alive. He could plan his escape later.

Sure enough, the next morning the men who had survived the night and could stand upright were chained into a grid twenty men wide and twenty men deep and marched off naked out of the valley.

John found himself walking along next to a man named Tom Milmer, one of the other Englishmen serving in the Earl of Meldritch's army. John and Tom did not talk as they walked past the piles of decapitated bodies that littered the valley and the bodies of drowned comrades strewn along the edge of the icy Oltu River. John calculated that more than twenty-five hundred of the three thousand troops in the Earl of Meldritch's army had been slaughtered in the valley the day before.

On and on they marched, the men trying to huddle together as closely as possible in an effort to keep their naked bodies warm. The first night John was surprised to find that the Turks provided them with a meal of lamb stew. He had not expected to be served good food along the way. Then he realized that they were probably in for a long march and their captors needed them to keep up their strength. But why? That was the question on John's mind, and John was sure that it was also on the mind of every one of his fellow captives.

The captured men marched together for three more days until they reached a town on the banks of the Danube River near the southern border of Transylvania. It was obvious that hundreds of Turkish soldiers were stationed there, and as the captives were marched through town, people jeered and threw stones at them.

Finally the men were led to a compound, where their chains were unlocked and they were given coarse tunics to wear. It felt good to be wearing clothes again. More food was available to eat, and doctors were there to attend to the sick.

All of this was fine except for one thing: the men still had no idea what was going to happen to them next. John had hoped that they would be sold back to Western slave merchants, who would free them for a price, but that was not very likely now, since they were deep in Turkish territory.

The days dragged into weeks, and it was a whole month before the men had any change in their routine. Then one morning their guards led them to big tubs of water and gave each man a cloth covered with oil of pine tar. The cloths were to be used to scrub their bodies clean of the lice and tiny insects that had taken up residence in the crevices of their skin.

John felt invigorated scrubbing himself clean, until he noticed that the men's coarse tunics had been taken away and the captives were left naked once again. When they were clean, the men were again lined up and chained together. This time they were led into the center of town, where each man was unchained and then rechained to a stake in the ground. John's stomach heaved; this was a slave market.

Once each man was chained to a pole, the Turkish officers interested in bidding for the men inspected them. They poked and prodded the men and opened their mouths to check their teeth. John watched in horror as Tom Milmer became indignant at this process. When an elderly Turkish officer tried to look into Tom's mouth, Tom struck the officer. The officer immediately stepped back, drew his scimitar, and felled Tom with one swing.

Seeing what had happened to his comrade, John suffered in silence through the indignity of being inspected like a horse. Several of the officers interested in bidding for John wondered whether he was really as strong as he appeared to be, and they had him and several other of the prisoners unchained and taken aside. There the men were made to wrestle each other, as well as to lift weights to show off their strength. When the demonstration was over, the men were chained up again and the bidding process began.

When the sale of the prisoners as slaves was over, John had fetched the highest price of the day. He had been sold to a man named Pasha Timor, the governor of Cambia (Bulgaria).

Following the sale, John was given a loincloth and a prickly woolen cape to wear and was taken to his new master's quarters. The following day the rivet was cut, and the metal ring around John's neck was removed. It felt good to have it off. This ring was heavy and constantly chafed raw the skin on John's neck. With ring removed, John was placed on a donkey, and then new chains were fitted to his wrists and ankles. Two guards mounted their horses, took the reigns of the donkey, and led John out of the city. They headed south for days on end. The journey was uncomfortable for John perched on the donkey's back, but he consoled himself with the fact that at least he was not being made to walk the distance on foot.

When the two guards stopped and made camp for the night, it was John's duty to prepare the food and serve it to them. If any food was left over when the guards were done, John was allowed to eat it. If nothing was left, he went hungry, which he did on a regular basis, as his guards seemed to have insatiable appetites.

After many days of riding, the men came to the city of Constantinople, the capital of the Ottoman (Turkish) Empire. Constantinople, once the capital of the Roman Empire, had been captured by the

Turks in 1453. The city was spread over seven hills around a harbor, and everywhere John looked he saw signs that Constantinople was now a Muslim city. The domes and minarets of mosques could be seen in every direction. But there were also still plenty of signs that the city had once been the most important Christian city in this part of Europe. Churches abounded everywhere, though they were no longer used for Christian worship but as storehouses and workshops and for other practical purposes. The city also showed plenty of evidence of its Roman heritage. The hippodrome still stood, and games were held there each week, and many smaller arenas were dotted around that were used for various forms of entertainment. In addition, the great Roman aqueducts that had supplied the city with water for centuries still stood and continued to bring fresh water to Constantinople. It was all quite magnificent, but John was in no frame of mind to admire the city. He felt humiliated and apprehensive about what might be in store for him now that he had arrived in Constantinople.

John was taken to a large house built of red stone and was handed over to the care of a group of slave women. While eunuchs guarded the door, the slave women bathed John, slathered him in perfume, and dressed him in women's clothes. When this was done, another slave entered the room to pluck out his eyebrows and paint on false ones with henna. It was one of the most humiliating experiences of John's life. John was a soldier, and now here he was, dressed in a woman's clothing and having his eyebrows plucked. John began to wish he had been killed that night back in the Oltu River valley in Transylvania.

As John endured having his eyebrows plucked, he looked closely at the slave girl doing it. She was unlike any of the other slave women. Her hair was blonde, her eyes were green, and her complexion was pale. "Are you English?" the girl finally whispered to John in a London accent.

"Yes. My name is John Smith," John quietly replied. "What's yours?"

"Elizabeth Rondee," the girl replied. "We will talk later."

With this conversation a tiny bit of hope crept back into John's heart. An English girl might be able to help him escape, or better still, perhaps they could escape together.

An hour after having his eyebrows plucked out and new, thin ones drawn on, John was lying prostrate on a tiled floor. In front of him was his new mistress, Lady Charatza Tragabigzanda. John soon found out she was extremely bored and had decided that he would entertain her and her guests by acting like a maidservant.

Having to perform in such a manner only served to pile up the degradation that John already felt. How he longed to be back wearing his own clothes. The only thing that kept him going were the small snippets of conversation he was able to have with Elizabeth. He learned from her that she was the daughter of an English diplomat who had been serving in Portugal. The entire family had been on a return voyage to England when Muslim pirates attacked their vessel. Elizabeth had to watch as the pirates killed everyone else aboard. For some reason the pirates had spared her life, and she was eventually taken to Constantinople, where she was sold for a high price to Lady Charatza. Elizabeth had been in Constantinople for about a year, she said, and in that time she had never left the house.

Elizabeth's story made John sad and angry, but he knew that if he lost his temper, he would be put to death. So he watched and waited. But his hopes for a joint escape were dashed when he learned that Elizabeth had been sent away to serve Lady Charatza's cousin in a faraway city in Morocco, in North Africa.

Not long afterward John found himself on the move. His mistress sent him to her brother Timor's house in Cambia. As he traveled along the shores of the Black Sea, John wondered what lay in store for him next. At least, he told himself, he was wearing men's clothes once again. And his eyebrows were growing back. He hoped that his days as a chambermaid were over.

When John finally arrived at Pasha Timor's estate in Cambia, he soon found that the man who had originally bought him at the slave market was a cruel master. At the estate John took his place among slaves from all over Europe who found themselves in the same unfortunate circumstances. The slaves toiled in the fields from sunup to sundown seven days a week. The smallest offense was met with a lash from the overseer's whip, and the person was given no food that night. John tried to stay focused on escaping, but he could not see any way that this could be done. Timor had placed another riveted ring around his neck, one he could not take off without help. And even if he did make a run for it and got the ring off his neck, he was still easy to identify as a foreign slave. He spoke little Turkish and wore fieldworkers' clothes. Besides, the penalty for trying to run away was death by torture, something that John was willing to risk only if there was a chance that he might actually get away.

Then, on a cold day in February 1604, the decision about whether or not to run away was taken out of John's hands. To stay would mean instant death. Fleeing was his only hope.

Chapter 7

Escape

Crack. Crack. The two hits from the riding crop sent searing pain pulsing through John's body. John awoke in an instant from his slumber on a pile of straw to the angry glare of Pasha Timor yelling abuse at him in Turkish.

John had been a slave now for over a year, and this chilly morning his overseer had sent him off alone to a field about three miles from Pasha Timor's castle to thresh rye. John had toiled away for several hours, using a heavy, wooden batlike tool to thresh the grains of rye from stalks of the plant. Every so often the straw piled inside the small barn beside the threshing floor beckoned him, and since he was not expecting to get checked up on for hours, he had decided to lie down and take a short nap. He lay down and moments later was sound asleep.

Pasha Timor continued to hurl abuse at John and hit him twice more with his riding crop. John's anger quickly boiled over. Without thinking, he jumped to his feet, grabbed the heavy, wooden bat he had been using to thresh the rye, and struck it across the side of Timor's head. The pasha stumbled, and John struck him across the side of his head again. Bleeding heavily, the pasha fell to the ground. Suddenly John realized what he had done: he had killed his master, and for that he would be brutally tortured to death. But John was not going to let that happen to him. He had to think fast.

Moving quickly, John stripped off Timor's clothes and hid the pasha's body under the pile of straw. He then pulled off his coarse, woolen tunic and dressed himself in the pasha's clothes. He could do nothing to hide the metal ring around his neck, and he knew that if he were spotted, the ring would give away the fact that he was a runaway slave. He would just have to take his chances. John mounted his dead master's horse and, once he had settled himself into the saddle, galloped off.

The next question John had to address was what direction to head in. He knew that he could not go west, because all of the territory to the west was under the control of the Turks. Neither could he go south, because he would be heading into Turkish-controlled land in that direction too. Finally he decided that he should head in a northeasterly direction, toward Russia. Like most people in Western Europe, John knew little about the place, as Russia was an isolated country that shunned contact with the outside world and was deeply suspicious of strangers. For all John knew, his fortunes could be worse there, but at least the Turks did not control Russia, and John thought that with luck he could make it there alive.

John rode for hours, being careful to avoid both Turkish military patrols and any people he saw, whether they were slaves or freemen. Long after the sun had gone down, John stopped to sleep for a few hours in a thicket at the edge of a field. He crept into a farmer's barn and stole some grain for his horse to eat, and before the sun was up the next morning, John was on his way again.

For the next sixteen days John traveled in this manner, stealing food along the way for him and his horse to eat. He traveled through the eastern reaches of Transylvania and then through Moldavia, which was also under Turkish control. Finally John crossed into Russia, where he breathed a sigh of relief. At least now the Turks were not going to catch him and torture him to death for killing his master. But he wasn't so sure about the intentions of the Russians. People fled when they saw him coming, and the gates to the many towns he passed were barred to him.

Once in Russia John began to head east along the north coast of the Black Sea and then along the edge of the Sea of Azov. Finally, almost three weeks after fleeing, he came to the city of Rostov, situated at the mouth of the Don River. As John approached the wall that surrounded Rostov, a group of soldiers rode out from the city and arrested him. John could not speak or understand a word of the language they spoke, and for a few moments he thought the soldiers were going to kill him on the spot. But eventually one of them grabbed the reins to John's horse and led him and the animal into the city.

John was not taken to jail, as he had expected, but was led to the residence of the city's governor, Baron Reshdinski. To John's relief, the baron could speak French, Latin, Greek, and Turkish as well as Russian. John's clothes were in tatters by now, and he was grateful when Baron Reshdinski led him into his residence and invited him to sit down. Then, alternating between French and Latin, John told the baron his tale of woe about being captured and sold into slavery.

Baron Reshdinski listened intently to all John had to say. "I like you. You speak well. And I am sorry for your treatment at the hands of the Turks. Although an outsider, you are welcome to stay here in Rostov, and I think you will find the people will treat you better than the Turks did," he said when John was done talking.

John let out a deep sigh of relief at these words. He was not going to be killed or made a slave by the Russians. And although John later learned that Baron Reshdinski had a reputation for being cruel to the people he ruled over, the baron showed nothing but kindness to John. He called for a blacksmith to remove the metal collar from John's neck, and then he had his barber trim John's hair and beard. He also provided John with some new clothes and had a servant lead him away to have a bath.

This was the first bath John had had in months, and the water soaking his skin felt good, though he found the Russian soap hard to take. It was so caustic it began to peel off areas of his skin.

The day after his arrival in Rostov, John took a walk to explore the city. In some ways Rostov was just like other cities in Europe. Some of its streets were lined with magnificent houses where the rich lived. John noted that any European nobleman would be happy to live in these houses. But other streets were lined with nothing more than mud huts, where the poor lived, and John decided that the poor areas were worse than any he had seen in Europe. What intrigued him the most, though, was the design of the city's numerous churches, which were unlike anything he had encountered before. With minaret-like steeples topped with bulbous, balloon-like roofs, the churches reminded him more of the Muslim mosques of Constantinople than the Christian churches of Western Europe and England.

Later that day John dined with Baron Reshdinski and his family. As he sat at the table ready to eat, he smiled to himself when he saw the enormous platters of food that servants carried out from the kitchen. It was more food than he had seen in years. John ate heartily, washing his food down with a number of glasses of the baron's best wine. As he ate, John could scarcely take in how his circumstances had changed. Just three weeks before he had been a slave, working from before sunup till after sundown seven days a week, with little food to eat, no blanket, and only the cold ground to sleep on. And now here he was, the honored guest of the governor of Rostov in Russia.

After a stay of nearly three months in Rostov, it was time for John to be on his way. Baron Reshdinski's niece, Camallata, was traveling north by caravan to Moscow, the Russian capital, and John decided to go north with the caravan. He said goodbye to the baron, thanked him for his kindness and hospitality, and was soon on his way to Moscow.

Moscow turned out to be much different from Rostov. The city was located in the middle of a pine forest on both sides of the Moskva River. Compared to Rostov, the city was drab and uninviting. The most imposing structure in the place was the Kremlin palace, a huge fortress surrounded by a high stone wall in which the tsar of Russia lived and from which he ruled the country. Although the rest of the city seemed dreary compared to the Kremlin, Moscow, since it was the capital, bustled with people. The streets were crowded with soldiers, diplomats, government officials, and local merchants.

As much as John would have liked to explore Moscow the way he had explored Rostov, armed guards prevented him from leaving the small apartment that Baron Reshdinski had arranged for him to stay in. When he protested, he was told that foreigners were not permitted to roam through the streets of Moscow at will.

After several weeks cooped up in his room, John decided that it would be best to return to Rostov. From Rostov, Baron Reshdinski arranged for a group of armed Cossacks to accompany John to the

Dniester River, Russia's border with Hungary. When they reached the river, John crossed it and rode on alone over the Carpathian Mountains. He had no idea what he would find on the other side of the mountains. If the fighting between the Austrian army and the Turks was still going on, he would rejoin the fight. And if it had ended, he would go in search of Prince Zsigmond of Transylvania to collect the annual pension he had been promised for defeating the three Turkish challengers in the three duels at Orastie.

As it turned out, John learned that an undeclared truce was in place between the Turkish and the Christian armies and that Prince Zsigmond was in Graz, Austria, visiting the Archduke Ferdinand. John set out immediately for Graz. As he made his way through Hungary, many people recognized him as the hero of the duels at Orastie and the sieges of Oberlimbach and Alba Regalis, and they offered him food and a room in which to sleep on his journey. John was thankful for the gratitude and hospitality of the people. It made the trip to Graz much easier.

When he finally reached Graz, John learned that Prince Zsigmond had moved on to Prague in Bohemia. John set out right away for Prague, but when he got there, he learned that the prince had moved on to Leipzig in Saxony. John hurried there, and this time he managed to catch up with Prince Zsigmond. And to his great delight, John's old commander, the Earl of Meldritch, was traveling with the prince. John had assumed that the earl had been killed in the fighting in the Oltu River valley in Transylvania where the Turks had captured him.

The earl told John his story of escape. When all had seemed hopeless in the battle, several of his officers had taken him aside and hidden him in some bushes. Then, after darkness fell, they had led the earl out of the valley to safety.

Prince Zsigmond and the Earl of Meldritch gave a great banquet in John's honor. At the end of the banquet, Prince Zsigmond presented John with a coat of arms. Now with his own coat of arms, John was entitled to write the word *Esquire* after his name. The prince also gave John a purse containing one thousand ducats, to which the Earl of Meldritch added another five hundred ducats. Prince Zsigmond also signed a safe-passage pass for John to use on his trip through Europe until he reached England. A safe-passage pass required the princes and kings who ruled other European countries to show courtesy and honor to bearers of such passes as they traveled through their territory.

With his safe-passage pass, coat of arms, and purse of ducats, John set out from Leipzig for Italy. He stopped in the city of Siena, Italy, where he happened to meet the Bertie boys, who were vacationing there. The men enjoyed a wonderful reunion, and John spent many hours regaling Peregrine and his wife, or more correctly, Lord and Lady Willoughby, and Robert Bertie with stories of his adventures since he had left Lincolnshire to go and fight the Turks.

From Siena Robert decided to accompany John to France, where they traveled the countryside for several weeks. After Robert left to return to England, John decided that it was time to see Spain, which until recently had been England's archenemy.

In Spain John visited the cities of Bilbao, Madrid, Toledo, Cordova, Seville, and Cadiz. He found these cites beautiful and the Spanish people warm and friendly toward him. John found that he liked nothing better than to sit in local taverns and talk to the people. It was during one of these conversations in a tavern in Cadiz that he was reminded of Elizabeth Rondee, the young English slave girl he had befriended back in Lady Charatza Tragabigzanda's household in Constantinople.

John was talking with a Portuguese captain, who told him that directly across the Strait of Gibraltar, the narrow opening to the Mediterranean Sea that separated Spain from North Africa, lay the country of Morocco. John recognized it as the place where Elizabeth had been sent to serve Lady Charatza's cousin, a pasha who ruled over the area for the Turks. As John plied the Portuguese captain with questions, he learned that this man, Mahomet ben Arif, lived and ruled from the town of El Araish, located on the Atlantic coast about fifty miles southwest of Tangier. Two forts set on the steep hill above El Araish guarded the town. The first fort dated back to Roman times and was strictly a garrison, but the second fort, called La Cigogne, had been built twenty-five years before by the Portuguese and was armed with cannons and catapults. The fort of La Cigogne was where Mahomet ben Arif and his family lived.

Over the next several days John learned as much as he could about El Araish from other sea captains who had visited the place. Armed with this information, John began to formulate a plan to rescue

Elizabeth. The plan took several months to pull together, but in September 1605 John set sail on a Spanish privateer for El Araish. Aboard the ship with him were eight mercenaries he had hired for the rescue attempt. Two of the mercenaries were French, two were English, and four were Spanish. Loose-fitting, fir-trimmed capes concealed their armored breastplates and weapons.

When the ship arrived in El Araish, John played the part of a rich and powerful pasha who ruled over Turkish-held territory in Eastern Europe. The eight mercenaries followed along, pretending to be his servants. In Turkish John announced to the harbormaster that he had come to pay his respects to Mahomet ben Arif and present him with a gift. The harbormaster provided the men with horses, and then John and his men made their way up the winding trail that led to La Cigogne.

At the fortress Mahomet ben Arif welcomed the men warmly and set a feast before them. After they had eaten, John retired to a private room with the pasha to talk while his men sat and drank with the pasha's armed guards.

John presented Mahomet ben Arif with what he explained was a valuable ring. In fact, the ring was a cheap imitation that John had purchased in Spain. A smile spread across the pasha's face as he accepted the ring and admired it. Still speaking in Turkish, John then cautiously asked, "Is it true, as I have heard, that you have an English slave girl in your household?"

Mahomet ben Arif did not answer the question. He just kept admiring his new ring.

"Ah, since I heard the rumor, I doubted that it was true," John said cunningly.

This comment spurred a response from the pasha. He admitted that he did have an English slave girl.

John laughed. "No, you are just saying that," he said. "An English slave girl is a rare thing."

"I have such a girl. I will send for her so you can see for yourself." With that Mahomet ben Arif barked orders for the girl to be brought to him.

A few minutes later Elizabeth Rondee appeared before them. Her appearance had changed little since Constantinople, but she did not appear to recognize John in his disguise.

John professed to the pasha that he spoke a few words of poor, fractured English and asked if he might speak to Elizabeth. The pasha agreed. Then, speaking in English, John quickly told Elizabeth who he was and that he had come to rescue her. Elizabeth was so shocked that she let out a gasp and tears formed in her eyes. John could see that Mahomet ben Arif had become suspicious, and before the pasha could call any of his guards from the next room, John pulled out a concealed knife from under his cape and jabbed him.

As Mahomet ben Arif curled over, Elizabeth let out a scream. This brought the pasha's ten guards rushing into the room. Right behind them were John's eight mercenaries, who pulled out their hidden swords. A vicious fight began. A few minutes later it was all over. All of Mahomet ben Arif's guards were either dead or so seriously wounded that they could not call for help, and one of the Spanish mercenaries was also dead. John took off this man's cape and hat and placed them on Elizabeth, and then the nine of them hurriedly left the room.

"Quick," John called as they hurried across the courtyard toward their horses.

They were mounting their horses when a pistol shot rang out, and a voice called for the guards to close the gate to the fort.

"They are on to us," John said, spurring his horse.

The escaping posse galloped toward the gate. The startled guards had no time to close it before John and the others roared through. Outside the fort the escapees formed into a single line, with John bringing up the rear. Elizabeth was positioned in the middle of the line. The nine of them made their way down the narrow trail as quickly as they could to the harbor at El Araish, where a boat was waiting to row them out to the ship. They had just climbed aboard ship when a group of soldiers from La Cigogne galloped up to the water's edge. The men aboard the privateer worked feverishly to get the sails hoisted and set before they could be captured. They were nearly done with the job when a barrage of cannon fire erupted from La Cigogne. Cannonballs crashed into the sea all around them, but none hit the ship, and soon they had managed to sail out of range.

"Thankfully their aim was not very good," John said matter-of-factly to Elizabeth as the ship headed out into the open water of the Atlantic.

It wasn't long, though, before a fleet of Turkish ships emerged from the harbor at El Araish to give chase. Fortunately for John and the others, the captain of the privateer was a skilled sailor. This, added to the fact that the privateer was better designed and more nimble in the water than the Turkish ships, meant that the captain was quickly able to outmaneuver their pursuers and leave them behind. The following day the ship docked in Cadiz, Spain, with a grateful Elizabeth Rondee a free woman.

Being a gentleman, John decided to accompany Elizabeth all the way back to London and see what new adventures awaited him there.

Chapter 8

A New Year
and a New Project

When John sailed up the Thames River into London on October 4, 1605, his arrival caused a sensation. He had been away for over four years, and in that time he had become a legendary war hero whose exploits were spoken about throughout England. Not only that, he arrived home with a beautiful English girl at his side whom he had rescued in a daring raid against a Turkish stronghold in Morocco.

Once back in England, Elizabeth went to live with her aunt and uncle in the country, while everyone wanted to hear of John's adventures in Europe. Tavern patrons bought him endless rounds of beer in exchange for his captivating tales.

Within a week of arriving home, John visited his friend Richard Hakluyt to tell him all about what he

had seen in Russia, a country to which few Englishmen had traveled. He also regaled the Prince of
Wales for hours with tales of fighting the Turks, and
he had an audience with the new king, James, and
his plump wife, Anne. Queen Elizabeth had died two
years before in 1603, and her cousin, King James
VI of Scotland, had ascended to the English throne,
becoming King James I.

John did not return home to Lincolnshire until
winter. He saw no need to rush back there, because
while he was away, his mother had died, and he was
not particularly close to his brother or sister. When
he finally did arrive back in Lincolnshire, John was
struck with the dull lives his siblings lived, and
although he had been through many hardships in
his travels, he was grateful that he had seen more
of the world than anyone else he knew. The visit to
Lincolnshire was a quick one, and John was glad to
be back in London for Christmas.

When he got back to London, John was immediately caught up in the excitement of New Year cele-
brations and a new project. His friend Richard
Hakluyt had been busy helping to found the Virginia
Company of London. For years Richard had been
advocating the establishing of English colonies in
North America. In 1584 he had published a book
on the subject titled *Discourse of Western Planting.*
In the book he laid out his reasons why he believed
that English colonies were necessary in North America. First, such colonies would serve as ideal bases
for attacking Spanish interests in the New World,
and they would stop both Spain and France from

establishing their own colonies in North America. Both countries had tried with little success to establish permanent colonies there. Second, English colonies in North America could serve as a place where the unemployed of Britain could go to find employment. And third, America was a land rich in natural resources that could be used for trade.

With these goals in mind, the Virginia Company of London was established and given a royal charter by King James. The company was a commercial venture with a plan to explore and settle North America, to find and bring back as many treasures as the people could locate, and to convert the native people to Protestant Christianity. John was captivated by the idea of conquering North America for England, and he invested five hundred pounds of his savings in the company. He also went a step further: he volunteered to be a part of the first wave of Virginia Company adventurers to go to North America.

Although John was not of noble birth, his reputation was high enough to win him an influential role in the expedition. Three ships were to be purchased and sailed across the Atlantic Ocean to America, and John was asked to join the three men who would captain these vessels as they prepared for the mission.

The commodore of the fleet was Captain Christopher Newport, and John liked his straightforward manner from the first time they met. It was obvious to him that Captain Newport knew his way around ships and the sailors who manned them. John could not say the same about Captain John Ratcliffe, who proved to be charming one moment and nasty the next. The third captain was Bartholomew Gosnold, who, although the youngest of the three captains, had made a successful voyage to the New World and back in 1602.

While he was busy planning for the expedition, John was surprised to be summoned to the Tower of London to meet with the great explorer Sir Walter Raleigh. Sir Walter, who had enjoyed the favor of Queen Elizabeth, had tried unsuccessfully to establish an English colony on Roanoke Island, off the coast of Virginia (today's North Carolina). King James, however, did not have a very favorable opinion of Sir Walter Raleigh and had had him arrested and locked up in the Tower of London on charges of treason that were flimsy at best.

At the Tower of London, John was led to Sir Walter's cell and let in. The space inside the cell was cramped, but Sir Walter Raleigh did not seem to mind, and he welcomed John warmly. John was drawn to Sir Walter, and the two men became instant friends, spending many hours together discussing the future of England. Sir Walter believed that it all came down to whether England was willing to colonize the New World. The Spanish and Portuguese had carved out for themselves colonies in South and Central America. The Spanish had also established outposts in Florida, on the North American continent, and the French were busy laying claim to territory in the north of the continent. According to Sir Walter Raleigh, it was imperative that the English lay claim to the territory between these two powers, thereby establishing England as a major power in the known world. John nodded in agreement as he listened.

"I hear that the Virginia Company of London plans to found a colony on Chesapeake Bay in Virginia," Sir Walter said.

"That is correct," John replied.

"It is a splendid location," Sir Walter continued. "That is where I had intended for my colony to be established, but one of my captains disobeyed my orders after setting sail and deposited the colonists on Roanoke Island instead."

John again nodded; he knew the story well. In 1585 Sir Walter Raleigh had sponsored an expedition to establish a colony in North America. One hundred seven men set out by ship and were deposited on Roanoke Island. But things had not gone well, and when Sir Francis Drake happened by with a flotilla of ships, he took the bedraggled survivors aboard and transported them back to England.

A second expedition consisting of 150 colonists was dispatched to establish a new colony on Chesapeake Bay, which was deemed to be a much more suitable location for a colony. However, the Spanish pilot of the fleet decided that it was too late in the year to sail north to Chesapeake Bay and instead dropped off the colonists at Roanoke Island. Unfortunately, England's struggle with Spain at the time had stopped ships sailing across the Atlantic to resupply the colony. When a ship finally did reach

Roanoke Island in 1590, the people found the colony
deserted. The inhabitants of the Roanoke colony had
disappeared, never to be seen again. Their disap-
pearance was a mystery that no one had been able
to solve.

"I wish you well in your endeavor, and may God
speed," Sir Walter said as John left his cell.

"Thank you," John said respectfully.

John and the three captains kept busy with their
preparations, and eventually they purchased three
seaworthy ships for the voyage across the Atlantic
Ocean. The first vessel they bought was the *Susan
Constant,* a relatively new one-hundred-ton square-
rigger. Captain Newport pronounced the vessel a fine
flagship and assumed the right to command it. The
second ship the men acquired was the *Godspeed,*
which was older and half the size of the *Susan
Constant.* Lastly the *Discovery,* a twenty-ton pinnace
(a small, flat-sterned vessel often used as a tender
for bigger ships) was purchased and assigned to
Captain Ratcliffe.

Once the vessels were all lined up alongside the
dock in London, the real work began. John took an
active role overseeing the provisioning of the ships
for the voyage. He inspected everything that came
aboard, aware that merchants often tried to pass
off inferior goods and provisions to ships. Among
the food stores that were loaded aboard were kegs
of sugar, prunes, raisins, and spices, and barrels of
pickled meat, salt pork, fish, and smoked bacon.
Since flour often spoiled during a voyage, rice and
oatmeal were loaded aboard instead. Stores of wine

were also loaded aboard to drink on the voyage, as was water, which was to be used only for cooking and drinking. Bathing would have to wait until the ships reached foreign shores.

Meanwhile the investors in the Virginia Company of London began to name other men who would join the expedition. These men included Edward-Maria Wingfield, a gentleman investor in the company, whom John thought was slow-witted and lacked coordination, and George Percy, the Earl of Northumberland's younger brother. The earl made it known that he hoped that a long voyage would cure George of his drinking and gambling habits. To help George and the other colonists with their spiritual needs, the company appointed the Reverend Robert Hunt, along with the son of a baronet, Gabriel Archer.

As John was introduced to the men one at a time, he began to wonder how they would ever form a team. None of them had any real idea about what lay ahead for them in America, and John knew that all of their lives could very well rest on how fast and how well they worked together. Other men, but no women, were added to the expedition party, allaying some of John's fears and bringing the ratio of men with "working skills" to half the total number of men in the party. There were bricklayers, carpenters, stonemasons, surgeons, a drummer, and four adventure-seeking boys.

By the time the three ships were ready to weigh anchor and set sail, an expedition party numbering 105 people had been signed up and were ready to risk their lives for the chance of colonizing a foreign land for England and Protestantism.

On New Year's Day 1607 all the members of the Virginia Company of London gathered at Westminster Abbey to take communion and listen to three sermons, one of them preached by the Reverend Hunt, the expedition's chaplain. Following the service, those setting sail for North America made their way to the dock at Blackwall, on the Thames River, where the three fully laden ships waited for them. Speeches followed, and then a sealed box was ceremoniously given to each captain. Each box contained an identical set of papers that outlined what to do once the expedition party made landfall, what the group's mission was to be in the New World, and, most important, the names of the seven men the directors of the Virginia Company of London had decided should govern the new colony. Such information was to be kept secret until the group set foot in North America. John assumed that this was so that no one would try to undercut the authority of the captains while they were aboard ship. He hoped that the carefully thought out plan would not prove to be a mistake.

Suddenly the rumble of thunder filled the air, and Captain Newport cut the speeches short and ordered the crews on deck and the passengers aboard the ships.

John was allocated to sail on the *Susan Constant,* as were the highest-ranking members of the group, except for the other two captains. The three captains ordered their ships' sails unfurled, and with no further ado, they set sail for the coast of North America. Of course they had to negotiate their way down the Thames River first and then around the coast of England to reach the open water of the Atlantic Ocean.

The next day, January 2, 1607, John Smith's twenty-seventh birthday, the ships sailed out of the mouth of the Thames River, headlong into a raging storm. They tried to make headway against it, but despite the best efforts of the captains and crew, the attempt proved fruitless. The wind and waves tossed the ships about, making life miserable for everyone aboard. Finally Captain Newport gave the order for the ships to heave to, and the ships dropped anchor in an area known as the Downs, just off the coast of Kent. For the next month they laid at anchor there, in sight of the English coast, waiting for a break in the weather.

It was a trying time for all aboard. The ships continued to pitch and roll as they bobbed at anchor, causing many aboard to get seasick, among them the Reverend Hunt, who looked so ill that John began to fear he might die. The close quarters aboard ship did not help the situation, and often tempers would fray and boil over into arguments and fights that other members of the expedition had to break up. John soon found himself embroiled in one of these arguments.

Edward-Maria Wingfield was a charter investor in the Virginia Company of London, and his father had been the godson of Queen Mary. Wingfield was traveling to Virginia aboard the *Susan Constant* with two servants. He came across to people as an overly confident and pompous man with an overinflated view of his superiority and position. In fact, his demeanor particularly irritated John, who was not a person to put much store in a man's social standing. After the ships had been at anchor for a week, Wingfield became impatient and began to agitate for turning back and returning to the comforts of home to wait for the weather to improve. Several of the other wealthy gentlemen adventurers aboard the ship took his side and also began pressuring Captain Newport to give the order to return home. Their actions infuriated John, who wondered why they had set out on the voyage in the first place if they wanted to turn around and run home when things got a little tough.

In no uncertain terms, John made his feelings known, and he watched in quiet bemusement as Wingfield turned white with rage at being spoken to in such a forthright manner by a commoner. The atmosphere on board the *Susan Constant* grew tense until the Reverend Hunt, still deathly ill, clambered off his bunk and settled the matter, siding with John in the argument. Despite the fact that he had been seasick for days, the Reverend Hunt told Wingfield and the other gentlemen adventurers that he would not embrace, even for a minute, the idea of turning back now that they had set out on the voyage to Virginia, even if two weeks after setting sail they were still within easy sight of the coast of England.

John was grateful that the Reverend Hunt had taken his side in the dispute, though he was sure that he had made enemies of Wingfield and some of the other rich and powerful men aboard. It would not be too long before John discovered just how far these new enemies would go in their efforts to get even with him.

After the ships had been at anchor at the Downs for six long weeks, the wind finally turned favorable, and the three ships weighed anchor and set sail once again. Before long they had passed through the English Channel and slipped out into the open water of the Atlantic Ocean. But the six weeks that they had been at anchor had given John some serious doubts about the future. After sizing up his fellow colonists, he wondered whether they would all even make it to the New World, let alone set up an English outpost together there once they arrived.

Chapter 9

The Long Journey

Once the ships reached the Atlantic Ocean, Captain Newport headed them in a southwesterly direction down the coasts of France and Spain. Two weeks after setting sail from the Downs, they reached the Canary Islands, located off the west coast of North Africa. There they stopped and took aboard more water for the journey. In sailing south they had left behind the cold of Northern Europe and were now enjoying the balmy warmth of the tropics. John, like most of the others traveling on the ships, now spent most of his time on deck, enjoying the sunshine, but that privilege was soon to be taken away.

Leaving the Canary Islands, Captain Newport picked up the prevailing easterly wind, and soon the three ships were racing along across the Atlantic Ocean.

While the sailing conditions were pleasant, rela-
tionships aboard the *Susan Constant* were anything
but. The animosity that had festered between John
and Edward-Maria Wingfield boiled over three days
after the ships left the Canary Islands. The two men
bickered constantly, with Wingfield seeming to grow
angrier after each exchange. John knew exactly what
was infuriating the man. It was his refusal to pay
Wingfield the respect he expected because of his
social position. But John could not help himself. He
believed that what recommended a man for respect
was the practical skills he demonstrated and not
the social stratum into which he was born. Wingfield might consider himself of high social standing
because of his birth, but as far as John was concerned, the man was a self-important buffoon, and
John did not easily tolerate such men.

John soon learned that to get even with him,
Wingfield and several of the other men of high
social position aboard the ship had been harangu-
ing Captain Newport with trumped-up stories of
how John was plotting an insurrection to take control of the ship. Finally Captain Newport gave in to
their demands and had John arrested and confined
below deck. John was angry and frustrated, but for
the time being, he could do nothing about the situation. Instead, below deck John poured his frustration into writing notes and journal entries that
outlined his grievances with those aboard the *Susan
Constant* and observations on how the expedition
was progressing. He wondered just how the men
would survive once they reached Virginia, with so

many of them aboard who seemed to act like spoiled children.

The diet on the trip across the Atlantic Ocean was a monotonous mix of hardtack biscuits, salt pork, and weak beer. John, even though he was under arrest, had been in much worse situations before, and he encouraged the people he encountered below deck to spend more time working and less time grumbling around the meal table. As good as his advice was for the long-term success of the expedition, it only won him more enemies than friends aboard ship.

Finally, one month after setting out from the Canary Islands, the ships reached the islands of the Caribbean. The first island they sighted was Martinique, which they sailed past, and the following day they dropped anchor off the island of Dominica. At Dominica they replenished the water and food supplies aboard the three ships and then sailed on. John, who was now allowed to venture up on deck during the day, had to content himself with viewing the islands from the poop deck of the *Susan Constant,* wishing he could go ashore and explore, as many others aboard did.

From Dominica the ships sailed on north past the islands of Maria Galante and Guadeloupe until they reached the island of Nevis. On Nevis everyone aboard the ships, including John, went ashore. John was delighted to again set foot on land. Once everyone was assembled on the beach, the group marched inland. They had to hack their way through the dense jungle with swords and axes. As the group slashed their way along, a number of men kept watch with muskets at the ready for any Carib raiding parties that might try to attack them. The Caribs were the fierce Indian tribe that inhabited the other side of the island. There were no attacks, and after heading inland for about a mile, the men reached a valley in which was nestled a crystal-clear spring. Here the men stripped off their clothes and bathed. Three months of dirt and grime soon floated away as John enjoyed every moment of his time bathing.

After they had washed, the group headed back to the beach. On the way back, however, another argument broke out between John and Edward-Maria Wingfield. The argument grew so intense that when they reached the beach, Wingfield took a rope and threatened to have John hanged on the spot as a traitor. Fortunately cooler heads prevailed, and John was not hanged. Instead he was ferried back to the *Susan Constant* and once again incarcerated.

The three ships anchored off the island of Nevis for six days so that the crew could rest before sailing on. While anchored there, a group of men caught a 280-pound turtle, which the crew cooked and served to those aboard the *Susan Constant.* But when someone shot one of the giant iguanas that roamed about the island, the crew drew the line and refused to cook and serve it. John had to admit that the turtle tasted better than he had expected, and he would have liked to have tasted the cooked iguana.

From Nevis they sailed on in a northwesterly direction, past the islands of St. Croix, Vieques, and Puerto Rico, until they came to the island of Mona, nestled between Puerto Rico and Hispaniola.

On Mona the ships took on more fresh water, and a group of gentlemen adventurers from the ships went inland on a hunting expedition. John watched them go, wishing he were free to join them. How he longed to be ashore once more, armed with a musket and stalking prey. However, when the bedraggled members of the hunting partly finally stumbled back to the beach hours later, John was glad he had not been with them. He listened as the men recounted what had happened. They had apparently misjudged the effect the tropical heat would have on them during the arduous six-mile trek inland to hunt and had taken no water with them. In addition, there was no water to drink along the way. As a result, the men quickly became dehydrated. Eventually one of the men, Edward Brookes, collapsed at the side of the hunting track. The men could do nothing for him, and he soon died. By then the rest of the men were too weak and dehydrated to find the strength to bury Edward's body, so they left him where he fell. Edward Brookes was the expedition's first fatality.

After the men from the hunting party had drunk pints of water to rehydrate themselves and had eaten to get their strength back, the ships sailed on. They stopped briefly at the nearby island of Monito, the last Caribbean island they visited. On April 10, 1607, they set sail north for Virginia.

The spirits of those aboard the ships were high as the men began the last leg of their voyage. The long trip across the Atlantic Ocean was behind them, and they had rested and replenished their food and water supplies as they island-hopped their way

through the Caribbean. Now the end of the long journey was in sight.

Four days after setting out on the final leg of
their trip, a storm began to brew as the ships sailed
off the coast of Florida. Captain Newport hoped to
outrun it, but luck was not on his side. John
watched as black clouds formed on the horizon.
Things grew more ominous each minute until by
midafternoon it had become as dark as twilight
around the ships. For the next week a huge storm
whipped up the sea that pounded away at the ships.
Huge waves washed across the decks of the three
vessels, taking valuable equipment and stores with
them in the process. Most of those aboard the ships
were violently seasick, though not John Smith. As a
result, John was pressed into service helping
Captain Newport sail the *Susan Constant*.

After a week, when the storm finally abated,
John watched anxiously as Captain Newport took
soundings to determine the depth of the water
beneath them. The news was devastating: the water
was over one hundred fathoms deep. The only con-
clusion the captain could draw from his depth
reading was that the storm had blown the ships
farther out to sea than he had expected. Unable to
accurately determine his position, Captain Newport
gave orders for the three ships to head in a northwesterly direction. He explained that by sailing in
this direction they would eventually intersect the
coastline of North America. And once they had
determined their position in relation to the coast,
they could head north or south to Chesapeake Bay.

For three days the ships headed northwest, but when the men still had not sighted the coastline, Captain Newport called the captains of the other two ships to a meeting aboard the *Susan Constant* to discuss what they should do. At the meeting John Ratcliffe, captain of the *Discovery,* argued that they should all return to England, where they could take on fresh supplies and start out again for Virginia. A number of the gentlemen explorers aboard the *Susan Constant* agreed with this position. But Captain Newport was unsure as to whether it was the most prudent course of action.

Some of the other gentlemen aboard spoke up in favor of pressing ahead on their present course, as did John Smith. John argued that if the ships returned to England, many of those aboard would desert the expedition. More colonists would then have to be recruited, postponing a return trip for some time. As well, the investors back in England would not be very happy if the men gave up now without trying a little harder to find the coast of North America. Not only that, some of these investors might decide to remove their money from the Virginia Company of London. The only course of action was to keep pressing on. To drive his point home, John ended by saying, "Those of you who want to turn back now are cowards. Why, even the eunuchs I encountered in the Ottoman Empire were more man than you."

This was a comment designed to shock and scorn those who had argued for turning back, and that is exactly the result it had. After weighing the matter, Captain Newport decided that they should continue on in their search for the North American coastline. However, many of the gentlemen explorers aboard the *Susan Constant* were offended by John's remarks, and Captain Ratcliffe stormed off the ship back to his own vessel.

In the morning the ships continued their journey, this time heading directly west. But they were soon overtaken by another fierce storm. Fortunately this storm lasted only a day, and rather than trying to sail the ships in it, Captain Newport decided to furl the sails and let the vessels drift with the storm. That night as he climbed into his hammock to sleep, John wondered what the next day would hold.

The following morning, April 26, 1607, John awoke to the yell of a lookout bellowing, "Land ho!"

John scrambled from his hammock and headed up on deck. Captain Newport had climbed the rigging to see for himself, and a group was gathering at the railing. The morning sun at his back, John peered into the distance. Sure enough, there on the horizon he spotted land. One hundred sixteen days after setting out from London, the ships had finally made it to the coast of North America.

"It's a peninsula, with a broad forest on it," John heard Captain Newport call from his vantage point high in the rigging.

Everyone aboard cheered, and for a moment all disagreements between the members of the expedition melted away. They had reached North America. It was time to build a new colony together.

As it turned out, the land they had sighted was the coastline of Virginia. It was not long before the three ships were sailing into Chesapeake Bay, where they dropped anchor at a place they named Cape Henry, in honor of one of King James's sons.

"They've picked a landing party, and you're not on it," one of the cabin boys informed John as soon as the sails of the *Susan Constant* had been furled.

John grunted. He was not surprised. The excitement of sighting land had worn off quickly, and the gentlemen explorers on board had decided to keep him under arrest on the ship. And although their decision disappointed him, John decided to wait it out. Eventually, he was sure, they would need his expertise and would let him go.

Longboats were lowered into the water, and thirty men climbed aboard them and began rowing toward the shore. John lined up on the deck with the others, waiting to see what would happen when the party landed. The men standing around him had differing opinions. One suggested that the Indians would attack the men as soon as they set foot ashore. Another man thought that the natives would greet the sailors warmly and lead them to a city made of gold, much like the Aztec cities in Mexico that had netted the early Spanish explorers so much gold. Still another man thought that wild animals, the likes of which they had never before seen, would attack the landing party. No one knew for sure what would happen. As it turned out, none of these scenarios proved true.

When they reached the shore, the men in the landing party beached the longboats, stowed the oars, and turned to wave to those on the ships. Then John made out the silhouette of the Reverend Hunt saying a prayer for the landing party. Undoubtedly the Reverend Hunt was thanking God that they had reached Virginia with only one life being lost along the way.

When the prayer was over, the men disappeared into the dense forest that crept up almost to the water's edge. Everyone aboard the *Susan Constant* settled down to wait for their reappearance. When the men finally emerged from the forest several hours later, they were sprinting toward the beach.

John narrowed his eyes and peered toward the shore. He could make out arrows whizzing past the heads of the men as they tugged the longboats into the water and jumped aboard. Captain Newport and several of the other men aimed their muskets and fired them into the forest. Then John saw another volley of arrows and heard screams from the longboat closest to shore.

John watched intently as the boats bobbed their way back to the ships, and soon the members of the landing party were being helped up and over the sides. Two men, Gabriel Archer and Mathew Morton, had been wounded in the attack by a small group of Indians. Gabriel had been shot with arrows through both of his hands, while Mathew had an arrow embedded in his groin. The ship's doctors cleared a space on the deck where the two injured men were laid. The injured men were given several swigs of whiskey each to calm them down before the arrows were removed and their wounds dressed.

As the sun set over Chesapeake Bay, lookouts were posted on each ship to watch for approaching Indian canoes.

The gloomy mood of the new colonists changed when Captain Newport strolled onto the deck, carrying the sealed metal box that contained the Virginia Company's instructions for what to do once the ships reached Virginia. The captain signaled the other two ships to send over as many of their men as possible, and soon a crowd had gathered on the deck of the *Susan Constant.* All eyes were on Captain Newport as he broke the seal on the box and pulled out several sheets of paper. The captain quickly scanned the papers and then began to read aloud.

> JAMES, by the Grace of God, King of England, Scotland, France and Ireland, Defender of the Faith, &c. ... do therefore, for Us, our Heirs, and Successors, GRANT and agree, that the said Sir Thomas Gates, Sir George Somers, Richard Hackluit, and Edward-Maria Wingfield, Adventurers of and for our City of London, and all such others, as are, or shall be, joined unto them of that Colony, shall be called the first Colony; And they shall and may begin their said first Plantation and Habitation, at any Place upon the said-Coast of Virginia or America, where they shall think fit and convenient, between the said four and thirty and one and forty Degrees of the said Latitude; And that they shall have all the Lands, Woods, Soil, Grounds, Havens, Ports, Rivers, Mines, Minerals, Marshes, Waters, Fishings, Commodities, and Hereditaments, whatsoever, from the said first Seat of their Plantation and Habitation by the Space of

fifty Miles of English Statute Measure, all along the said Coast of Virginia and America, toward the West and Southwest, as the Coast lyeth, with all the Islands within one hundred Miles directly over against the same Sea Coast;...And shall and may inhabit and remain there; and shall and may also build and fortify within any the same, for their better Safeguard and Defense, according to their best Discretion, and the Discretion of the Council of that Colony; And that no other of our Subjects shall be permitted, or suffered, to plant or inhabit behind, or on the Backside of them, toward the main Land, without the Express License or Consent of the Council of that Colony, thereunto in Writing; first had and obtained.

A separate document went on to name the seven men who had been appointed to the council by the Virginia Company of London to take charge of and lead the new colony. The first three names on the list were predictable: Captain Christopher Newport, Captain Bartholomew Gosnold, and Captain John Ratcliffe. These three names were followed by the names of the three highest socially ranked men in the expedition: George Kendall, John Martin, and the Virginia Company's single largest investor, Edward-Maria Wingfield. That left one more member for the council, and all heads turned when Captain Newport read out the name of John Smith.

John resisted a smile, although he would have liked nothing better than to burst out laughing.

Many of the gentlemen explorers on board had scorned him for much of the voyage, and now he had been named as one of the seven leaders of the new colony.

Captain Newport did not comment. Instead he continued on reading the orders from the Virginia Company of London. These instructions included such practical matters as how to choose a settlement site so that they would not have to waste time unloading the ships and then have to move everything to the site. The site they chose should be at least ten miles up a river so that they would not be vulnerable to Spanish attack. The instructions also allowed the colonists to keep the smallest ship, *Discovery*, with them, while the other two vessels were to return to England carrying a load of something commercial that they found in Virginia. The Company hoped that this cargo would be gold or precious stones. In addition, the colonists were to immediately put together a team of forty men to search for the Pacific Ocean, since the prevailing wisdom was that the continent of North America was probably no more than one hundred miles wide.

At the same time, the instructions admonished the new colonists to be careful not to offend the natives. Instead they should try to trade with them and eventually win them over to Christianity.

The last instruction stated that no one could leave the colony without permission of its president and council, and that all mail would be read before being sent on to England to ensure that no negative reports were sent home. The public back in England was not to be discouraged about progress of the colony in Virginia.

John did not get much sleep that night. Questions swirled in his mind. Had the Indians been scared by the musket shots when they attacked the landing party, or would they be emboldened by having managed to shoot two of the colonists with their stone-tipped arrows? Would the new colony survive? Would the colonists disappear without a trace as the colonists on Roanoke Island had seventeen years before? Would they be massacred before they established the new colony and their bodies left as a warning to future English colonists? And if none of these things came to pass and they were unmolested by the Indians, would the new colonists be able to cooperate well enough with each other to build a fort and feed themselves so many miles away from England? John then turned his thoughts to another matter: would he be allowed to take his rightful place on the ruling council, or would some of the other council members find a way to keep him off it? He knew that these questions had no immediate answers. He knew only that everyone would have to wait and see what would happen.

The following morning it was obvious that the six other council members had held a meeting without John and had made some decisions. They had elected Edward-Maria Wingfield as their president, and Wingfield had immediately reminded the colonists that they needed to locate a site for the new settlement and at the same time begin the search for the Pacific Ocean and as many treasures as they could find. The Virginia Company of London was a commercial venture, and those who had invested in the company wanted to see an immediate return on their investment. To aid in this process, all the able-bodied men were divided into two groups. Twenty-five of them, including the ships' carpenters, would assemble the shallop, a two-masted, gaff-rigged vessel designed for sailing in shallow water, that had been stowed in pieces on the deck of the *Susan Constant,* while a second group of about fifty men would explore the inland area on foot.

Once again John was ordered to stay back on the *Susan Constant.* This frustrated him greatly, since he was one of the best fighters in the group and would be an asset if the group was attacked by Indians.

As it turned out, when the land team returned to the ships, they reported coming across a fire with oysters cooking over it, the Indians having hurriedly abandoned it when they heard the Englishmen approaching. That was the closest the team had come to an encounter with the local people.

Over the next two weeks, John became increasingly frustrated with his lot. Parties of men left the ships each morning to explore the shoreline and hinterland of Chesapeake Bay, but he was not among any of them. And although he should be one of the decision makers of the new colony, he was still under arrest. Each night the men who had gone ashore would come back with tales of Indian villages they had seen and of the pristine pine forests they had walked through, while John saw none of it.

On May 13, 1607, the six active men on the council decided on a site for their new community. The site was located on a swampy peninsula about thirty miles up a river, which they named the James River, in honor of King James. The men decided to name the settlement they were about to establish Jamestown, also in the king's honor. The site had two main features that recommended it. First, it would be easy to defend by land, since only a narrow land bridge connected the peninsula to the mainland. And second, the water around the site was very deep, with trees growing right to the water's edge. This meant that the ships could tie up to the trees, and off-loading their cargoes would be a much easier task.

Now, at last, every available hand was needed to help establish the new outpost. John was released from arrest so that he could help unload the ships, clear land, and pitch tents. As John helped to unload barrels of rice and oatmeal and kegs of sugar from the holds of the ships, his mind was busy trying to think of a way to win over the other colonists so that he could take his rightful place on the council.

Chapter 10

Building Jamestown

John put down his ax and wiped his brow. It was hard work clearing enough land on which to build twenty cottages, and he had been chopping down trees and splitting logs all morning. As he reached for a mug of water to drink, John spotted movement in the long grass to his left. Calmly he gulped two mouthfuls of the water and put down the mug. Then, trying to appear as if he were resuming his work, he reached down and picked up the ax. Just then two Indians showed themselves. The pace of John's heart quickened as he stared at the man directly in front of him. The man was tall, with copper-colored skin that was painted in red, blue, and green dyes. Half of his head was shaved, and the hair on the other half was tied in a knot on top of his head. The man was wearing an animal-skin loincloth.

John did his best to look friendly and unafraid, though he felt angry because he did not have any weapons other than the ax with him. Colony president Edward-Maria Wingfield had decreed that all guns and ammunition were to be left in their shipping crates and that no walls or other defenses were to be built around the new settlement. He argued that this would demonstrate to the Indians that the settlers had come in peace. John, on the other hand, felt that it would send quite a different message: that the settlers were weak and easy to attack.

Now, as the two Indians approached, John tried to look calm. Both men held their bows out in front of them, which John took as a sign that they had come in peace. And so they had. Through a series of hand signals, John guessed that the men were messengers from a powerful chief who was soon going to pay the colonists a visit.

Sure enough, the following day over one hundred Indians, each man armed with a bow and arrows, descended on Jamestown. With them was Chief Wowinchopunck. The Indian men divided into two rows, and the chief then pointed to a deer they had brought with them. The chief appeared to want the colonists to cook the deer for a feast.

The colonists had already agreed to cook all of their meals in one common area and had lined a hole in the ground with rocks to make a fire pit. A fire was hastily lit in the pit while the deer was being dressed for roasting over the flames. Meanwhile an uneasy silence fell over the Indians and the colonists. The two groups were about the same in number, but the Indians had the clear advantage of available weapons. John cursed to himself; he hated being in such a vulnerable position, especially when he might have been able to change things had he been on the council. Still, he realized that it was too late to worry now. He would just have to watch and see how things played out.

The sun was well past its zenith by the time the deer was cooked. The meal was tense, and everyone seemed relieved when Chief Wowinchopunck indicated that it was time to go. As the Indians walked away from the settlement, one of them reached down, grabbed an ax, and ran. A colonist sprinted after him, tripping him up and punching him hard in the face. Chief Wowinchopunck's face turned to thunder at the treatment meted out to one of his men and signaled for the rest of them to hurry away.

John was troubled by Chief Wowinchopunck's visit, but President Wingfield stayed in a jovial mood, assuring the colonists that they were doing the right thing by not showing strength.

After the visit by the local Indians, everyone had plenty of work to keep busy with. Once the trees were cut down, the logs split, and the stumps removed from the ground, it was time to start building the structures that would form Jamestown. Stonemasons, bricklayers, and carpenters set to work constructing the cottages that would house the men. These cottages had high-pitched thatched roofs and consisted of two rooms: a living room and a bedroom large enough to sleep four to six men.

The cottages built for the gentlemen adventurers were slightly larger and were designed to sleep only two men. The cottages were erected facing a common area where the communal fire pit was located.

Work on the cottages progressed well, and as it neared completion, the builders began to focus on their next task—building the settlement's three communal buildings: a church with a steeple, a storehouse to hold their food supplies and other goods, and an arsenal in which to store their barrels of gunpowder and crates of muskets.

The church was quickly taking shape, and the foundations for the storehouse and arsenal had been laid out when President Wingfield ordered Captain Newport to pick twenty-two men to take with him on an inland exploration trip that could last up to two months. John was appalled by this decision, as it would reduce the population of Jamestown by nearly a quarter, leaving the new settlement vulnerable to attack. But Edward-Maria Wingfield was determined to find either the Pacific Ocean or gold and gems, and he hoped to find all three, if possible.

The only good news, as far as John was concerned, was that Captain Newport picked him to join the expedition inland, along with four other colonists: Gabriel Archer, to keep a log; Thomas Wotton, one of the settlement's two physicians; George Percy; and John Brookes. The other seventeen members of the party were all seamen from the three ships. John was concerned about the men who were staying behind at Jamestown. He could see that Captain Newport had picked the hardest workers of the group to go with him, but no one else had seemed to notice that detail.

The twenty-three men set out for points unknown at noon on May 21, 1607, in the shallop. They sailed about eighteen miles up the James River before dropping anchor for the night. The following morning two canoes filled with Indians appeared in the mist. The Indians were friendly and indicated through gestures that there was a waterfall at the end of the river and then a great mountain range, on the other side of which was another ocean.

The news greatly cheered the men in the expedition party. The men were convinced that they would reach the Pacific Ocean within a week. The two canoes paddled alongside the shallop as it sailed on up the river. Every now and then the natives would shout greetings to someone on the shore.

Over the years, Peter Plancius in Amsterdam and Richard Hakluyt and Henry Hudson in London had given John pointers on how to go about drawing an accurate map of an area. Now as the men made their way up the James River, John put their advice to good use, drawing a map of the river and surrounding countryside as they went.

Around a bend in the river the Indians yelled more greetings to people on the shore, and this time the Englishmen were invited to come ashore.

Nestled under some trees along the riverbank was a small Indian village. The people of the village warmly welcomed the twenty-three Englishmen.

They laid out mats on the ground for them to sit on and set out food for them to eat. They served the men fish and venison and bread made of ground corn. They also brought nuts and berries for them to feast on. John recognized most of the berries—strawberries, mulberries, and blackberries—which all grew in Europe. But the Indians also laid out a strange blue berry that none of the men had ever seen before. Gingerly John put several of the berries in his mouth and ate them. He liked what he tasted. The berries had a mellow, sweet taste that was very pleasant, and John quickly reached for some more of them.

As he ate, John peered around at the huts that made up the village. The huts were almost all the same. The walls were made of reeds that had been covered in tree bark, and the rounded roofs were made of thatch. The huts had doors but no windows, and mats covered the door openings. A number of the dwellings also had scaffold-like structures erected outside them, over which mats had been stretched to form a kind of veranda.

When the Englishmen had eaten their fill, the men of the village got up and entertained them with a dance. One man stood in the middle of a circle of men and began to clap in time. The other men then began to move their feet in unison as they danced around the clapping man. The Indian men had painted their bodies with bright-colored dyes, and their hair was shaved in the unique fashion of the two Indian messengers John had encountered back at the settlement over two weeks before. The Indian men were an impressive sight as they danced away. John was enthralled by the whole scene, and he watched the dance closely. He observed that while the men all moved their feet in unison, the gestures they made with their arms and faces were all different as each man expressed himself through the dance. The dance lasted for over half an hour, and John was amazed at the stamina of the Indians and their ability to dance so vigorously for such a long time.

Soon it was time for the expedition party to get back aboard the shallop and head on up the river. Before they left, however, the chief of the village insisted on providing the colonists with a guide named Nauiraus for the continuation of their journey upriver. John was delighted by this outcome, as it gave him plenty of opportunity to learn some local Algonquian words from Nauiraus, since Algonquian was the language spoken by Indian tribes of the region.

The James River began to narrow as the men headed on up it, until their voyage came to an abrupt end at the foot of a majestic waterfall. Captain Newport decided not to look for a way to carry the shallop overland to the top of the falls but instead decided to return to Jamestown and report what they had discovered so far. The men camped the night at the foot of the waterfall and held a church service the next morning, as it was Whitsunday. Then with pomp and ceremony, Captain Newport erected a simple wooden cross, bearing the inscription "Jacobus Rex [Latin for King James] 1607." He then made a proclamation that England claimed all of the land from there all the way to the Pacific Ocean. With the ceremony over, the men ate lunch together and then set out back down the river in the shallop.

On the return trip, John continued to learn Algonquian words from Nauiraus. John would point at an object, and Nauiraus would say the Algonquian word for it. John would then write the word phonetically in a notebook. Before long, he had learned enough words to say short phrases and then simple sentences in Algonquian. As John spoke the words and sentences to Nauiraus, Nauiraus would correct John's pronunciation and syntax.

The days went by pleasantly enough, and the tribes the Englishmen met along the way were friendly and interested in trading beads, mirrors, and other baubles for food. However, that all changed on Wednesday, May 27. John, who now understood some Algonquian, noticed it first. Instead of being friendly, the Indians who now paddled by in their canoes often seemed angry and rude. And finally Nauiraus made up an excuse and quickly parted company with the Englishmen.

By then the men were only hours from Jamestown, but every minute seemed to drag on as John began to wonder whether the Indians had turned on Jamestown. With each bend in the river, John worried about what they might find when they arrived back.

Finally the river took one final twist, and Jamestown came into view. From a distance everything looked fine, but as they sailed closer, John scanned the riverbank. First he saw a teenage boy lying in the mud with an arrow sticking out of his back. Then he noticed that the flimsy fence around the settlement had been trampled down, and clothes and food were strewn over the ground.

John felt sick to his stomach. Had anyone survived the Indian attack?

Chapter 11

Chief Powhatan

With a few strokes of the oars, the shallop pulled up beside one of the trees at the river's edge, and John, pistol in hand, leapt out. The other men followed him as he ran toward the settlement. As John neared the first cottage, several men emerged from inside it.

"We were attacked yesterday!" one of the men yelled. "Hundreds of them. If it had not been for Captain Gosnold, we would all be dead."

"Where's President Wingfield?" John asked, his pulse racing at the thought of unarmed men being attacked.

"In the end cottage with some of the wounded," came the reply.

John raced along the path to the end cottage, where he found ten men groaning from various arrow wounds.

"There's seven more in the cottage next door, and two men dead," President Wingfield said flatly. "We were overwhelmed—outnumbered—the forest is full of Indians."

John nodded. It was a fact that had been obvious to him from the moment the ships dropped anchor in Chesapeake Bay. But he had better things to do than argue with Edward-Maria Wingfield right now.

Everyone seemed to be being taken care of, so John left the cottage and wandered through the settlement. Apart from distant groaning, Jamestown was silent. The men who were unharmed looked as though they were in a trance. At last John found his friend the Reverend Hunt and asked him to explain exactly what had happened.

The Reverend Hunt did not have much to tell. No one had had time to count the number of Indians involved in the raid, but the Reverend Hunt guessed it to be about four hundred. The Indians stormed the settlement, knocking over the fence. The colonists ran to the newly completed storehouse for shelter, since none of them had any guns. Thankfully Captain Gosnold had been quick thinking enough to secretly lead a group of sailors out of the settlement. They rowed to the *Discovery,* anchored just off shore, and fired one of the ship's cannons at the village, hitting a large tree branch in the process. As the tree branch crashed to the ground, the Indian warriors turned and fled, carrying away with them one of their number who had been killed by a colonist's sword. All had been quiet since then, but as the Reverend Hunt explained, no one had the courage to leave his cottage, not even to go to the water's edge and retrieve the body of the boy who had been killed by an arrow.

John shook his head when he heard what had happened. "The cannon fire may have scared the Indians off once, but we can't rely on that every time we are attacked," he said. "It was the kind of surprise diversion that you can get away with only once or perhaps twice."

"Yes, I know," the Reverend Hunt replied quietly. "Providence has granted us a narrow escape, but we must find a better way to defend ourselves."

And that became John Smith's mission. John had said all along that the men should be armed at all times, and now everyone agreed with him, except for President Wingfield, who still believed that it was better to remain defenseless and at the mercy of the Indians.

Ignoring the president, John organized the healthy men to build a strong palisade around the village. At the same time he tested each man's ability to shoot a pistol and a rifle. Much to his surprise, he found that many of the men had never touched a gun before. He set about drilling the men every morning on the rudiments of handling, maintaining, and firing a gun. While this was going on, the Indians continued to attack Jamestown, though in small raiding parties. One colonist was killed, along with a dog, and several men were injured in these raids.

During this time John noticed that he was the one to whom the members of the Jamestown community came for advice on how to protect themselves. He was not surprised when, on June 10,

1607, the men of the community pressured the council to have him take his rightful place on the leadership team. Apparently the council and President Wingfield had also taken note of John's natural leadership abilities, because they had him take the oath of office that same day.

Five days later John learned some important information about the Indians who were attacking them. Two Indian men arrived at Jamestown. In Algonquian they called "Wingapob! Wingapob!" which meant "Friend! Friend!" The two men were invited into the settlement, and one of them turned out to be Nauiraus, who had been their Indian guide on the trip up the James River. Nauiraus explained who the tribes were that were attacking the settlement. They were the Paspahegh (who claimed the land on which Jamestown had been built), the Weyanock, the Appomattoc, the Kiskiack, and the Quiyoughannock. However, Nauiraus explained, not all the Indian tribes in the region were against the Englishmen. He explained that the Arrohattoc, the Pamunkey, the Mattaponi, and the Youghtanund were their friends. And these tribes would try to intercede with the others to get them to stop their attacks on Jamestown.

As John listened to what Nauiraus had to say, he could immediately see the precariousness of the settlement's position. All the tribes that Nauiraus had named their enemies were their immediate neighbors, and those who declared themselves to be their friends lived the farthest away from Jamestown. John hoped that these friendly tribes would

be successful in interceding on their behalf and stop
the constant attacks the community was being sub-
jected to.

When he had finished overseeing the men as
they chopped down oak, beech, and white pine trees
to build the palisade around Jamestown, John, as a
member of the council, was faced with the impend-
ing departure of the *Susan Constant* and the
Godspeed. Both ships were scheduled to depart for
England on June 22. The investors of the Virginia
Company had made it clear from the beginning that
they expected shiploads of goods to be transported
back to England so that their sale could cover the
company's costs and, they hoped, provide a hand-
some profit. But since no precious metals or gems
had been found so far, the council had to think of
other profitable cargo to send home.

To fill the ships' holds, John visited several of
the friendly tribes Nauiraus had told him about and
traded with them, giving them trinkets and axes in
return for beaver and fox pelts. It was not the kind
of cargo that the Spanish galleons returning from
Mexico to Spain were carrying, but everyone hoped
it would placate the Company's investors back in
England.

The *Susan Constant* and the *Godspeed* sailed on
time for London, with Captain Newport promising to
do his best to be back at Jamestown in November
with fresh supplies. That was twenty weeks away,
and as the colonists watched the ships sail down the
James River, John tried to sympathize with those
who were saddened and afraid to be left alone. But

for his part, he was secretly glad to see the ships go. Now, at last, the colonists would have to pull together into a tight community to survive.

That is what John had hoped would happen. In fact, the opposite occurred. It soon became obvious that the best workers had been the sailors from the ships, and now that they were gone, most of the men could not be bothered to work. There were crops to weed and waterproof roofs to build, but John could not seem to motivate people to help him. He was astonished by this behavior, especially since summer would not last forever, and they all knew that it got cold enough in Virginia to snow in the wintertime. If they were to survive, the storehouse would have to be full of food. Yet even when their food stores began to dwindle and the men had to be rationed to half a pint of boiled barley and half a pint of wheat per person per day, they were still not motivated to rally round and begin gathering food supplies for the winter.

John conceded that the men's lethargy could be partly due to the hot weather. Virginia in July and August was certainly hotter than any day in England, and the men suffered from heatstroke if they stayed outdoors for too long. The hot weather also brought other problems, mainly with the water supply. When they had landed at the small peninsula where Jamestown now sat, it was spring, the time when the James River flowed swift and deep with water from the melting snow in the mountains. But by midsummer, the river's flow was greatly reduced, allowing the tidal water to flow farther upriver. As a result, the water in the river at Jamestown became salty and slimy and stagnant enough for a good crop of mosquitoes to breed.

By the beginning of August, the tainted water, lack of fresh food, and malaria-carrying mosquitoes had begun to take their toll. On the sixth day of that month, one colonist died from dysentery. Three days later another man died, followed quickly by another. Soon at least one death occurred each day. Those unaffected by dysentery had to nurse the sick, bury the dead, and stand guard at the palisade. It was all John could do to keep them at their posts. Then John himself fell sick with dysentery. He lay in his bed, lapsing in and out of consciousness, totally unaware that the entire colony was on the brink of collapse. A group of Indian children with arrows could have wiped them all out, but thankfully during this time no Indian attacks took place. In fact, the opposite occurred as Indians began arriving at the settlement with corn and venison to trade.

News arrived that Captain Bartholomew Gosnold had died on August 22, and John vaguely recalled hearing a cannon shot in his honor. Fortunately, the dysentery spared John's life, but by the time John was again aware of what was going on around him, forty-one of the other colonists, nearly half of the entire group, had died from the disease. The only member of the group who had not been sick with dysentery was President Wingfield, and John soon discovered the reason why. The president had let himself into the storehouse and taken eggs, beef, oatmeal, and liquor. While men were malnourished and dying around him, he secured the best food for himself. This infuriated John, who formed an alliance with two of the other councilors to have Wingfield removed from the presidency of Jamestown.

Tempers ran high as the surviving colonists blamed President Wingfield for their suffering. It was no surprise to anyone when John presented Wingfield with a signed order discharging him from his leadership role of the Jamestown community. Captain John Ratcliffe was made the new president in his stead. Wingfield was forced to stand trial for taking food and was convicted of the offense by twelve jurors and ordered to be kept locked up aboard the *Discovery* with George Kendall, who had also disobeyed the colony's rules.

As a result of the president's stealing, John was put in charge of watching over the storehouse and bartering with the Indians. This was an important task, perhaps the most important task in the colony at this time, because the Indians had stopped bringing food to barter and the colonists had less than a three-week supply of food left on hand.

Although no one liked the idea, everyone agreed that it would be best if John were to lead a group of colonists to the nearby friendly Indians' villages to see what they could barter. This left only thirty men in Jamestown to hold down the fort.

John was gone for seventy-two hours, and in that time he managed to cajole several tribes into bartering. He took both the shallop and the *Discovery* upriver with him, and soon both vessels were filled to overflowing with corn, beans, fish, oysters, and venison. On the way back downriver, the men stopped at a salt lick John had spotted on the earlier excursion with Captain Newport and dug up salt, which would be used to preserve the seafood and meat for the long winter ahead.

With John as their leader, the men made a triumphant entrance at Jamestown. The new food supply invigorated everyone, and the colonists set to work to prepare their tiny settlement for the coming winter.

November arrived, and with it driving rain, but no sign of Captain Newport or ships loaded with supplies. John heard rumblings around the settlement that some of the men hoped to return to England on the ships, or even take the *Discovery* and head for home on it. Nothing came of this, however, and John soon began making plans for a different voyage.

John was an explorer at heart, and since there was not much for him to do during the winter months, he decided to continue his search for the Pacific Ocean. He had concluded that it would be fruitless to try to climb the waterfall on the James River, since it would be almost impossible to haul the shallop to the top of it. He decided instead to concentrate on exploring the Chickahominy River, which branched off the James River several miles upriver from Jamestown, hoping that this river would provide an easier route west.

In early December John selected nine colonists to accompany him on the trip. The men climbed aboard the shallop and hoisted the vessel's sails.

They made good time for the first forty miles, until they passed Apokant, the farthest village up the Chickahominy River. Once they passed the village, the river narrowed until it was evident that they would not be able to take the shallop much farther. John gave the order to come about and head back down the river to Apokant, where he hired two Indians and their canoe to take him farther upriver.

The canoe had only enough room for John and two other people plus the two Indians. John chose a carpenter named Thomas Emry and a gentleman explorer named Jehu Robinson to accompany him. He was concerned about the seven men remaining behind, and he ordered them to stay in the shallop no matter what happened. With a final wave, John set out in the canoe.

When the men had paddled about three miles up the river, they decided to stop and cook their midday meal. While one of the Indian guides built a fire, John decided to explore inland for a mile or two. He motioned for the other guide to go with him, while Thomas and Jehu stayed behind. John cautioned both men to keep their guns at the ready and fire them into the air at the first sign of trouble so that he could rush back to their aid.

John and the Indian guide set off into the woods. John's pistol was cocked and ready to fire at any tasty animal that crossed their path. Only fifteen minutes after setting out, John heard a yell from the riverbank but no shot. He surmised that the other guide had attacked his two companions. But just as he was thinking of what to do next, he heard a swishing sound, followed by a sharp pain in his thigh. He looked down to see an arrow protruding through the right leg of his pants. He spun around, and there stood two Indians with bows in hand and more arrows ready to fire at him. John leveled his pistol at them and fired. His shot missed, but the two attackers quickly scurried away.

The arrow embedded in John's right thigh had not hit the bone, and he grabbed it and pulled it out of his thigh. Searing pain shot up his leg, but he did not have time to worry about it. Immediately John began reloading his pistol, and as he did so, four Indians appeared from among the underbrush and shot arrows at him. One of the arrows went right through the sleeve of his heavy coat, but it did not pierce his arm. The Indians turned and ran after they had shot their arrows, and John fired his pistol after them.

After John had quickly reloaded his pistol, he grabbed the Indian guide and pulled him in front of him as a shield. But John soon realized that his plight was hopeless. He was completely surrounded by a band of hundreds of Indian warriors. John pulled the guide closer to him as he tried to think of what to do next. But the frightened guide made the next move. He called out to the Indians that John was not just any Englishman—he was a leader. When John heard the words, he knew that the guide had bought him some time, because according to local custom, a leader was to be captured alive.

John waved his revolver in the air and then pointed it at the Indian guide's head, calling out that he wanted to be allowed to return to the canoe at the riverbank or he would shoot the man. He then nudged the guide, and the two men began walking slowly back the way they had come. It was an uneasy standoff, and John was so intent on watching the Indians around him for any sudden moves that he failed to notice where he was placing his feet as he walked. As he took a step, he placed one foot down into the edge of a large, muddy quagmire. Suddenly he lost his balance, falling sideways and pulling the Indian guide with him. The two men soon found themselves neck deep in oozing mud.

The Indian warriors rushed in and stood around the quagmire, arrows at the ready in their bows. John waited for the razor-sharp stone tips of their arrows to begin raining down on him, but instead a well-built man with graying hair stepped forward. The guide quickly told John that the man's name was Opechancanough. The man was the chief of the Pamunkey Indian tribe and was one of Chief Powhatan's younger brothers. John had heard of Chief Powhatan, the powerful chief of a confederation of Indian tribes in the area.

Opechancanough stared down at John in the mud, and John knew exactly what he wanted—the pistol. The situation was hopeless. Both he and the Indian guide were sinking deeper into the quagmire. John finally handed over the weapon. Then powerful arms reached down and pulled him and the guide from the mud.

Standing, mud dripping from him, John thought fast. He knew that the local Indians were as infatuated as the English were with a man's rank and status in society. Mustering his still rather fractured Algonquian, he began to try to convince Opechancanough that he was indeed a man of rank and status. He also knew from observing the Indians since arriving in Virginia that they tended to think of anything they could not understand as being supernatural. As he spoke, he pulled his compass from his pocket, holding it out for Opechancanough to see. The chief was fascinated as he watched John turn the ivory case of the compass around in his hand while the needle continued to point in the same direction. Opechancanough took the compass himself and repeated the action.

John's efforts seemed to have paid off. Opechancanough appeared to believe not only that John was a man of importance in his society but also that he was a man with supernatural powers. Instead of having John killed, the chief and John marched on to a hunting camp several miles away. As they walked a group of warriors surrounded John, arrows cocked in their bows ready to shoot him if he made any wrong move. For his part John felt lucky to still be alive and decided to leave the matter of escape for a later time.

At the hunting camp John was allowed to wash the caked mud from his body and clothes, and then he was led into a tentlike lodge, where a fire blazed in the middle of the floor. He sat on a mat by the fire, and soon two Indian women appeared with platters of venison and bread for him to eat. John ate heartily, but there was so much food that he suddenly began to wonder whether the Indians were fattening him up to eat.

That was not the case. Mostly Opechancanough wanted information. Why had the Englishmen come to their land? Why had they built a fort? How long did they intend to stay? Why did the Englishmen have no women with them? On and on the questions went as John tried to give evasive answers to each new question.

After several days at the hunting camp, John was led on to another village. And after a few days at that village, he was led on to yet another village. This pattern continued on until December 30, 1607, when he was led into Werowocomoco, the village from where Chief Powhatan ruled over the confederation of tribes under his control. The village was located on the north bank of the Mattaponi (York) River, and until now no Englishman had ever laid eyes on the place, let alone on Chief Powhatan.

At Werowocomoco John was led into a large meeting lodge made of reeds and thatch. Since the lodge had no windows, it was gloomy inside. The only light came from the fire in the middle of the room and from the door opening. Once his eyes had adjusted to the light, John noticed a man seated on a mat on the other side of the fire. The man was clad in a robe made of raccoon skin and wore strings of pearls around his neck. John looked closely at him. He knew that this must be Chief Powhatan, but he found it hard to tell how old the man was. Yes, his hair was completely gray, almost white, but his physique resembled that of a man much younger.

Around the chief sat a number of females, most of whom John soon learned were Chief Powhatan's wives. But some of them were the chief's children, including a young girl of about twelve years of age whose name was Amonute but whom everyone seemed to call by her nickname, Pocahontas, which meant "playful one" in Algonquian. Pocahontas sat staring at John as her father began to question him.

Like his younger brother Opechancanough days before, Chief Powhatan wanted to know why the Englishmen had come to Virginia and settled in his territory. He also wanted to know why two of the ships had left and whether and when they would return.

In answer to the questions, John made up a story about how the three ships had been involved in a fierce battle with their enemy the Spanish and they had been forced to take shelter in Chesapeake Bay to repair their ships. Two had been repaired, but the one ship was still leaking, and they were working to repair it. The other two ships had left to get supplies, and when they returned, the Englishmen would finish the repairs and all sail away together back to England. John explained that in the meantime he had been on a trip to find the great ocean on the other side of the continent when he was captured.

John made up the story about the ships so as not to give the chief any information about Jamestown and its long-term goals lest Chief Powhatan decide to destroy the place. John thought it much better for the chief to think that it was just a temporary camp and soon would be gone.

Chief Powhatan held John's life in the balance, and John knew it, so he decided to raise the stakes. He told the chief that since he was a leader among the Englishmen, they would expect him to return to the settlement soon. If he did not return, the Englishmen would surely come looking for him, carrying muskets and coming in boats armed with cannons.

After hearing all John had to say, Chief Powhatan gathered together a group of advisers to decide John's fate. John sat nervously for several hours while the chief and his advisers talked heatedly among themselves.

Finally Chief Powhatan made his decision. He signaled to several warriors standing at the door of the lodge, and moments later the warriors rolled in a large, flat stone and set it in front of the fire. Two burly men then emerged carrying heavy wooden clubs. John felt his pulse quicken.

Several warriors grabbed John and pulled him forward to the stone. They forced his head down onto it and stood back as the two other warriors raised their clubs.

Chapter 12

Cheating Death

As John waited for the club to fall, he felt hair brushing against his cheek. He looked up to see Pocahontas laying her head on his. Suddenly there was complete silence. The club did not fall.

"Pocahontas, why have you done this?" John heard Chief Powhatan ask his daughter.

"I do not want him to die," she replied, lifting her head. "Father, I beg you to spare his life and give him to me."

Chief Powhatan sighed. "As you wish," he said. Then turning to the gathered crowd, he added, "There will be no killing today. Pocahontas shall have her way."

John felt strong arms lift him up and escort him to a hut, where he was bound and left alone. In the semidarkness he wondered what would happen next. Would Chief Powhatan allow him to return to Jamestown, or would he be kept at the village and made to obey Pocahontas's every whim? The answer came two days later when the chief appeared at the door of the hut, flanked by two hundred painted warriors.

"We are now friends," Chief Powhatan told John. "I will think of you like a son. You may return to your people. I will send men to escort you. All that I ask is that you give them two great guns and a grindstone."

John's heart soared. He was going to be freed, after all. He eagerly agreed to the terms of his release, and later that day he set out overland for Jamestown. Twelve men, including Rawhunt, one of Chief Powhatan's most trusted warriors, accompanied him on the march.

The group arrived back at Jamestown an hour after sunrise, on January 2, 1608. The sentries at the settlement looked stunned as John appeared at the gate. Nearly a month had passed since he had set out from Jamestown, and everyone assumed that he had been killed. Once safely inside the palisade at Jamestown, John learned that Thomas Emry and Jehu Robinson and one of the men he had left behind with the shallop at Apokant had been killed by the Indian guide. The rest of the men had escaped downstream in the shallop and had lived to tell the story of what had happened to them.

Understandably, no one at the settlement wanted the Indian escort party to stay at the fort any longer than necessary. John pointed out two three-hundred-pound cannons and told Rawhunt that he could have them. Rawhunt frowned as he realized that there was no way his group, or even one hundred men, could carry the "great guns" home. In fact, it had taken a mechanical hoist to lift them off the *Susan Constant* and place them on the palisade.

John tried to stay serious. "Tell Chief Powhatan that I offered you the guns but you were unable to remove them," he said. "To compensate I will give you axes and cooking pots, and mirrors for your women. I will also give you the grinding stone your chief asked for."

Rawhunt grunted. He knew that he was beaten, and this made John smile to himself. John had outwitted the great chief and resisted arming the natives with European weapons. He believed that swords, guns, and cannons must be kept away from the natives at all costs.

Once the escort party had been dispatched, it was time for John to catch up on the everyday life of the colony. Winter ailments and a shortage of food had taken their toll, and as a result only forty men were now left of the original one hundred five. In John's absence a number of the remaining men, including John Ratcliffe and Gabriel Archer, who had been appointed to the ruling council in John's absence, had begun planning to abandon the colony and sail the *Discovery* back to England. John put an immediate stop to this plan, which enraged President Ratcliffe, who retaliated by having John arrested for leaving Thomas Emry and

Jehu Robinson alone with the Indian guide, who had killed them both.

The charges were outrageous, and when the president could find no support for them in English law, he turned to the Bible and quoted from the book of Leviticus. The passage he quoted stated that an eye should be given for an eye, a tooth for a tooth, and a life for a life. Since John had been careless with the lives of two men, John Ratcliffe argued, he should lose his own life in turn.

The argument was flimsy and unjust, but the men were desperate to get John Smith out of the way so that they could sail home to England. Within twenty-four hours of being welcomed back to Jamestown, John had been sentenced to death by hanging.

All of this happened so swiftly that John was stunned, especially since he had just cheated death at the hands of the Indians, only to face it at the hands of his fellow countrymen. That night John sat down to eat what he imagined would be his last meal. But as he was eating, a trumpet warning sounded. A ship was sailing up the James River.

Suddenly everything was thrown into turmoil as men ran to the river's edge to see whether the ship was friend or foe. Cheers went up as a large British ensign was hoisted from the ship's mast. The vessel was the *John and Francis,* under the command of Captain Newport. Fresh supplies and reinforcements had arrived at Jamestown at last!

Captain Newport quickly sized up the situation at Jamestown and set John free. Of course John was delighted, and he was also delighted to have the sixty new colonists that were aboard the *John and Francis,* not to mention the food stores in the ship's hold. After a two-day holiday, everyone pitched in to help with the task of unloading the ship. Soon barrels of salt pork and preserved beef were being loaded into the storehouse, along with olive oil, butter, cheese, and beer.

No sooner had most of the ship's cargo been unloaded than one of the newcomers accidentally overturned an oil lamp, setting fire to his cottage. The fire quickly spread until it had consumed nearly every building in the settlement, including the newly stocked storehouse and the church.

This was a bitter blow for the community, but the Reverend Hunt helped John and the others to remain optimistic. Although he had lost his library of theological books along with the church, the reverend was thankful that no one had been hurt or killed by the fire.

After the fire had ravaged Jamestown, the people had nothing left to do but start rebuilding the settlement. The members of the community stayed aboard the *John and Francis* until new cottages were completed. Thankfully the ship's hold still contained some provisions, and better yet, Captain Newport told John that the *Phoenix* should be arriving any day. The two ships had set out from England together, but they had been separated in a severe storm as they approached Chesapeake Bay. Even if the *Phoenix* had been blown off course, it would not take many days for it to sail back to Jamestown. On board this vessel were fifty more colonists and stores of food.

In the meantime, Chief Powhatan had noticed the *John and Francis* at anchor in the river off Jamestown and sent word that he wanted to meet with Captain Newport and trade with him.

John, Captain Newport, and thirty men boarded the *Discovery* and sailed down the James River and up the Mattaponi River to Werowocomoco to meet with Chief Powhatan. The chief welcomed the men to his village, and with John acting as interpreter, he and Captain Newport began the process of trading. The Englishmen had brought hatchets, copper cooking pots, and various trinkets to trade for food. As was usual in the bartering arrangement, Captain Newport placed a hatchet before Chief Powhatan to see what the chief was willing to give for it. But Chief Powhatan approached things differently, catching Captain Newport off guard.

"Captain Newport, I am a great man, and it is not agreeable to me to trade in such a trifling way. You, too, are a great man among your people. Lay down together all the commodities you have brought to trade. What I like of these commodities I will take and compensate you what I think is a fair value for the items," Chief Powhatan said.

As John translated the chief's words, he wanted to scream "No, don't agree to it" to Captain Newport, but such a comment, or even a gesture not to do it, would arouse the chief's suspicions and put their lives in jeopardy. John just hoped that Captain Newport could see through what Chief Powhatan was trying to do. However, Captain Newport did not see the trap Chief Powhatan had set for him, and he agreed to the chief's proposal, laying out all the items he had brought to trade.

John fumed inside as he watched Chief Powhatan pore over the items. By the time the trading was finished, Captain Newport had managed to secure only a fraction of what he could have if he had traded the items one at a time. John decided that Captain Newport had paid a pound's worth of trinkets to get what John would normally have gotten for a penny's worth of trinkets. As the meeting drew to a close, John decided that he had to try to do something to save the situation.

While remaining outwardly calm but still fuming inside, John began to finger a handful of blue beads. When Chief Powhatan saw what he was doing, he asked about the beads.

"These beads are of a rare substance the color of the sky. They are most favored by the greatest kings in the world, and I could not possibly give them up," John told the chief.

Chief Powhatan pressed John to trade for the valuable beads. John kept putting him off, saying that the beads were too valuable, until Chief Powhatan was desperate to have them. By the time he was done, John had traded the beads to the chief for three hundred bushels of corn. The beads, of course, were worthless baubles, but John was satisfied that his efforts had saved the day's trading from disaster.

Once the corn and other goods were loaded aboard the *Discovery*, the Englishmen set out for Jamestown.

After bargaining with Chief Powhatan, Captain
Newport turned his attention to another matter—
finding gold. Although there was no evidence that
the precious metal was anywhere to be found
around Chesapeake Bay, John learned that Captain
Newport had promised the directors of the Virginia
Company that he would return with a shipload of
it. In preparation he had brought with him to
Jamestown two assayers and two goldsmiths, along
with enough buckets, pans, and shovels for everyone to participate in a gigantic scavenger hunt for
gold. President Ratcliffe and John Martin were carried away with the captain's enthusiasm, and John
found himself the only man urging a slower
approach. What use was gold, he argued, if they did
not have clothes to wear or proper protection from
Indian attack? Worse, Captain Newport vowed to
delay his leaving until gold was found, and the
sailors from the *John and Francis* were rapidly eating up the colony's new food supply. This was crit-
ical because the *Phoenix* had not arrived and was
presumed lost at sea with all hands on board.

Try as he may, John could not get anyone to listen to him, and the hunt for gold began. Day after
day the men trekked along the riverbanks, panning
for the elusive metal. Even though none was found,
Captain Newport was sure that some of the mud
and silt dredged from the bottom of the river did
contain gold, and he ordered barrels of it to be
loaded aboard his ship. It was early April before the
task was complete and Captain Newport was willing
to set sail for home. Learning of the upcoming
departure of the *John and Francis* for England,

Chief Powhatan sent along twenty turkeys and asked Captain Newport to exchange them for twenty swords. John was furious when he learned that the captain had consented to this request. The first European weapons were now in the hands of the Indians.

On April 10, 1608, the *John and Francis* set sail for England after being at Jamestown for three and a half months. John, for his part, was glad to see Captain Newport and his hungry sailors leave. And better yet, Edward-Maria Wingfield and Gabriel Archer were also aboard the ship. Their absence would cut down on the daily tension in the colony.

Ten days after the *John and Francis* had sailed for London, John was out cutting down trees with a number of colonists when an alarm trumpet sounded. John put down his ax and ran to pick up his musket, fearing that Jamestown was under attack from a band of Indians. He ran to the settlement, the other colonists following close behind him. Fortunately the colony was not under attack. Instead a merchant ship had just rounded a bend in the James River and was headed toward the settlement. The vessel was flying a British ensign from its mainmast, and as it got closer, John could see through his telescope the ship's name—*Phoenix.* The ship that had been presumed lost with all hands aboard had finally shown up. The residents of Jamestown excitedly ran to the river's edge to welcome the vessel.

Once his vessel was safely tied up at Jamestown, Captain Thomas Nelson of the *Phoenix* told John the tale of the previous four months. The storm that had separated the *Phoenix* and the *John and Francis* at the entrance to Chesapeake Bay had driven the *Phoenix* south and out to sea. The ship, in fact, had gone so far south that Captain Nelson had decided to head for the West Indies, where the ship and crew had wintered over. Finally, after three and a half months, the weather was stable enough for the *Phoenix* to continue on to its destination. While the ship was laying over in the West Indies, Captain Nelson had traded for food from the inhabitants of the various islands and so had not been forced to delve into the food supplies in the ship's hold.

This news delighted John. Not only was the *Phoenix* carrying fifty more colonists, whose labor could be put to good use, but also her hold was full of food supplies.

The day after the *Phoenix* arrived at Jamestown, the members of the colony set to work unloading the contents of her hold into the storehouse and building more cottages to house the extra colonists.

With this done, the colony set about adjusting to the new members and provisioning themselves for the next several months. Their efforts were made difficult, however, by visits from Chief Powhatan's men. Emboldened by the bartering of twenty swords from Captain Newport, the chief had sent along twenty turkeys to John Smith and asked that he exchange them for more swords. John refused to do this and sent the messenger away empty-handed, in the hopes that in the process he had not created a new enemy for Jamestown.

It now seemed that what Chief Powhatan could not trade for he was content to steal. Small groups of Indians began to infiltrate the settlement and steal weapons and implements. This infuriated John, who determined to make an example of anyone he caught stealing. Soon the colonists captured a dozen Indians on a raiding party to steal from Jamestown. John had them imprisoned and sent a message to Chief Powhatan, demanding the colony's property back in exchange for the men. The next day, two colonists who were foraging for food outside the settlement were taken prisoner by Indian warriors.

John decided to take action. He collected a small group of men, and they all set off upriver in the shallop. The first Indian village they came upon they burned to the ground and smashed the canoes that lined the riverbank. Then they returned to Jamestown, where John awaited Chief Powhatan's response. It came the following morning in the form of the two prisoners and a pile of stolen shovels left at the settlement's gates. Still determined to show the chief who had the upper hand, John released one of the Indian prisoners and terrorized the other eleven men, holding them at gunpoint and making threats of torture.

On the third day Chief Powhatan tried a new approach to appease John and the colonists. He sent Rawhunt and Pocahontas to ask for the warriors' release. The symbolism was not lost on John. Pocahontas had once asked that his life be spared, and now she was asking that he spare the lives of her kinsmen. John could do nothing but agree to let the captive Indians go.

Despite the circumstances of the visit, John was glad to see Pocahontas again, and he invited her to visit the settlement anytime she wished.

Soon afterward, on June 2, 1608, the *Phoenix* set sail down the James River. The vessel was headed back to England, carrying a full load of cedar shingles. Captain Nelson also carried with him many of the maps John had drawn of the area and a manuscript that John had written outlining his adventures in Virginia so far.

By now it was midsummer, and with so many hands busy tending to the crops they had planted to feed the community, John felt sure that he could be spared to continue his exploration of the Chesapeake Bay area. He chose fourteen men to accompany him, and they all set out in the shallop.

For the next seven weeks the men explored the inlets and waterways of the Chesapeake. As they moved north, they left the territory that Chief Powhatan ruled over and entered the territory of other Indian tribes. They also sailed a good distance up the Patawomeck (Potomac) River. As they went, John drew an accurate map of the territory they explored, marking in the names of the various tribes that lived along the rivers and bays of the Chesapeake.

On their way back to Jamestown, John decided to explore up the Rappahannock River. On the way back down the river, however, the shallop ran aground on a shoal in the river mouth. The vessel was stuck fast, and the men could only wait for a high tide to float the shallop free. Fish were abundant in the shallow water over the shoal, and the men passed the time fishing. Rather than use a fishing line, John contented himself with spearing the fish with his sword, a method he became very adept at. As he was doing this, a fish unlike any fish John had ever seen before appeared in the water beside the shallop. This fish was round and flat and had a long, spiked tail. To move, the fish undulated its body.

Intrigued by what he saw, John speared the fish—which he would soon learn was called a stingray for good reason—with his sword. As he lifted the creature impaled on the end of his sword, the fish spun around, flicked its spike of a tail, and embedded its tail an inch and a half into John's arm. The wound drew no blood but left just a blue mark where the stingray had pierced his skin. The pain, though, was more intense than anything John had ever felt before, and his whole arm and shoulder began to swell. One of the men applied some cream to the wound, but that did not seem to do any good. The pain in John's arm just grew more intense.

After two hours of lying in searing pain in the bottom of the shallop, John was certain he was going to die. "Go ashore and dig my grave," John ordered several of the men, "for I won't be long out of it."

The men did as he said, wading to a small island in the mouth of the river and digging a shallow grave.

The men watched dolefully as John writhed in pain. John himself knew it would be only a matter of minutes before they laid him in the hole they had dug. But the minutes turned into hours and slowly the pain John was feeling began to subside. John began to wonder whether perhaps he was not going to die after all! By late afternoon the pain had sub-sided almost completely, though John's arm was still tender and swollen. And there was more good news: the high tide had floated the shallop free of the shoal. The men rowed the boat ashore, where they lit a fire, and in a kind of poetic end to the day, John cooked and ate the stingray that had inflicted so much pain on him.

The next day the men set out for Jamestown. As always, John worried as he neared the settlement. He had never returned to find the place in a better condition than he had left it, and this time was no exception. When he arrived back, hatred for President Ratcliffe had reached an all-time high. John Ratcliffe had allowed too much of the settle-ment's food rations to be consumed, and he had ordered the men to stop all other work to build him a grand house in which to live. Some of the colonists were so angry with the man's blundering leadership that they were ready to lynch him. Others were in favor of ousting him from his position of leadership and installing John Smith as Jamestown's new president.

John was not eager to take on the position. He had seen enough to make him wary of taking on the supreme leadership of such a difficult group of people. However, it was obvious that President Ratcliffe had lost the respect of everyone in the community, and so John finally agreed to become the new president, on the condition that he could choose his own vice president. This was accepted, and Captain John Smith became president of Jamestown, naming Matthew Scrivener, one of the new colonists who had arrived on the *John and Francis* with Captain Newport, as his deputy.

One by one the members of the community stepped forward to congratulate John, but John felt no sense of pride in his new position. His only goal was to keep alive as many of the residents of Jamestown as possible until the next ship arrived from England.

Chapter 13

He That Will Not Work Shall Not Eat

The supply ship sailed into Jamestown far ahead of schedule in early September 1608. On board were two women and eight German and Polish workers, along with sixty other eager English colonists. John officially welcomed them all and then went aboard the ship for a private conference with Captain Newport. During the meeting the captain handed John a letter from the board of the Virginia Company of London. John broke the wax seal on the letter and unfolded it. As he read it, he felt his blood begin to boil. The letter contained three directives. One, that the ship, in order to make the voyage profitable, return to London with a freight worth two thousand pounds. Two, to find gold, or a route to the Pacific Ocean, or to find survivors from the Roanoke colony. And three, to go and crown

Chief Powhatan as a "subking" in the British Empire.

The demands of the letter were almost more than John could bear. How could the gentlemen of the Virginia Company send him such ridiculous orders? But the orders had to be obeyed in some way or another. John was particularly concerned about crowning Chief Powhatan as a subking. What would the chief make of such a gesture? Would it puff him up with pride or anger him? John was not sure, but since Captain Newport was determined to carry out his mission, he assembled a party of 120 men to visit Chief Powhatan and bestow the honor upon him.

John watched as Captain Newport set out with three barges laden with gifts for the chief, including a four-poster bed, a red cape, a washbasin, a pair of shoes, and, of course, a gold crown for the new "Tributary Prince of the Realm."

While the group was gone, John had a daunting task ahead of him. Captain Newport had brought seventy new colonists with him, including two women, one married and one single. For the first time, the colony was not an all-male group, and some of the rules had to change to accommodate the women. John and the council made it illegal for the men to curse or to relieve themselves in the bushes outside the fort. New outhouses were built for the latter purpose.

The eight German and Polish tradesmen who had arrived on the supply ship also added frustration to John's workload. The Polish men did not get along with the Germans, and neither group appeared to like the English. Against this backdrop, John was supposed to supervise the men as they set up a factory to produce glass, pitch, and tar. The added stress made John angry, but he did his best to provide samples of the new products for Captain Newport to take back with him to England.

Captain Newport and his men all returned to Jamestown safely, though many of the men doubted whether Chief Powhatan had any idea as to why they had all come to his village to put a metal band on his head. As soon as the group returned, John set out downriver with thirty men to cut down trees to make shingles to help fill the ship's hold. As far as he was concerned, the sooner Captain Newport and his hungry men left, the better off the colonists would all be.

When John and the men returned to Jamestown a few days later from their tree cutting, John's worst fears were realized. Chief Powhatan had cut off all trade with the settlement, claiming to be insulted once he had worked out that he was now seen as an underling to the English king.

Just as the first frosts of winter began to blanket the ground each morning, Captain Newport set out on the second part of his mission, to find something of great value in Virginia. He decided to search above the falls on the James River, but the barge he took with him upriver was much too heavy for the men to carry up to the top of the falls, and so the trip was soon abandoned. Captain Newport arrived back at Jamestown empty-handed and concerned at what the members of the board of the Virginia Company would say when they found out.

It was all too much for John, who wrote a scathing letter to his superiors in London, telling them how stupid he thought they were and how their outrageous ideas of instant wealth were putting the lives of the colonists in jeopardy.

Other lives were at stake as well. Captain Newport had banked on being able to barter for food with the Indians, but now that there was no communication with them, he had no way to feed his crew on the long voyage home. John finally allowed him to take most of the meager food supplies from Jamestown, and the ship sailed for London in mid-December. The best news of all was that John Ratcliffe was aboard the vessel, returning to England, John hoped, for good.

The situation was precarious once the ship left, and everyone rejoiced when word arrived from Chief Powhatan that he would indeed be willing to fill the colony's storehouse—for a price. The price he wanted was an English-style house to be built for him at Werowocomoco, a grindstone, fifty swords and guns, and a hen and rooster.

John sent back an envoy to agree to the terms immediately, though he had no intention of supplying the chief with swords and guns. He decided to work out how to deal with that situation later. Meanwhile, he sent the German glassmakers and two Englishmen to start work on the foundation of the house and to spy on Chief Powhatan's men at the same time.

A short while afterward, John ordered two barges loaded with the supplies necessary to build an English-style house, and on December 24, 1608, the barges left Jamestown for Werowocomoco, with the men celebrating Christmas along the way. On January 12, 1609, the barges reached Werowocomoco, where John found the chief in a good mood. The chief welcomed John and his men as they set to work building his bark-and-thatch home.

The work went quickly, though John could not shake the idea that Chief Powhatan planned to attack him if he let down his guard. Then the night before John was to return to Jamestown, Pocahontas appeared at the door of the lodge where the men were staying outside Werowocomoco. Risking her life, she had come to warn John that her father was planning to kill him and his men. Her father was sending dinner for them, but the warriors who were bringing the food had been charged with disarming John and his men and then killing them all. Pocahontas also warned John to be wary of the two Germans, as they had been secretly spying on him for her father. John thanked Pocahontas for the warning, and the chief's daughter disappeared into the night as quickly as she had come.

Eight burly warriors arrived at the lodge an hour later, bearing platters of cooked venison for John and his men to eat. The warriors explained that the meat was a gift from Chief Powhatan, and John and his men, their muskets at the ready, eyed them warily as they set the platters down.

The warriors tried to make small talk as they waited for the Englishmen to begin eating so that they could overpower them. But the wary Englishmen sat looking at their guests. Finally one of the warriors coughed and spluttered and said that it was too smoky in the lodge. He then suggested to John that he have his men extinguish the burning lengths of cord that smoldered beside the fire. The cords were used to ignite the gunpowder in their matchlock rifles. John recognized the warriors' plan in an instant, and he realized that the warriors must have picked up this piece of information from the Germans. With the burning cords put out, the warriors would then be able to overpower John and his men and kill them without having to worry about being shot in the process.

John laughed at the warrior's suggestion and, pointing to the fire in the center of the lodge, said, "The fire is much more smoky than each man's burning cord. Perhaps you should go outside, where the air is fresher."

The warrior shrugged his shoulders as if he did not understand.

Finally the warriors seemed to realize that the element of surprise was gone, and after a few minutes of both sides staring each other down, the warriors withdrew, leaving the men to eat the venison.

Throughout the night John posted guards to keep watch lest Chief Powhatan mount another attack to try to kill them. Fortunately the night passed quietly, and early the next morning the men set out downriver in a barge loaded with food stores Chief Powhatan had provided them as payment for the house.

When John got back to Jamestown, he received still another blow. His deputy, Matthew Scrivener, and ten other colonists had drowned on a short expedition to Hog Island, a small island located half a mile downriver from Jamestown.

To make matters worse, on Captain Newport's last voyage, a number of stowaways had traveled on the ship from England and had sneaked off it into Jamestown. The stowaways were rats, and now they had infested the settlement and eaten the few food stores that remained in the storehouse. Not only that, but the colonists, especially the newly arrived gentlemen explorers, had done little to help themselves while John had been away. As a result, many of the cottages were rotting in the damp climate, and most of the tools and a lot of the weapons were gone. John assumed that traitors among them had traded the tools and weapons with the Indians.

John had had enough. It was time for action, and he could carry out that action alone. Now that Matthew Scrivener was dead, only one council member was left, and he had one vote, while John, as president, had two votes. John called the community together and spelled out exactly how things were going to be from now on. He began in a loud voice: "I speak this not to all of you, for divers [some] of you I know deserve both honor and reward, better than is yet here to be had. But the greater part [of you all] must be more industrious, or starve, however you have been heretofore tolerated by the authority of the council.... You see now that power rests wholly in myself, you must obey this now as law, that he that will not work shall not eat (except by sickness he be disabled), for the labors of thirty or forty honest and industrious men shall not be

consumed to maintain a hundred and fifty idle loi-
terers.... There are now no more councilors to protect you."

John made it clear that he was prepared to follow through on his "He that will not work shall not
eat" policy, and the colonists got the message loud
and clear. Within three months they had pulled
together to build twenty new cottages, dig a well,
and plant thirty acres of crops. John also ordered
the colonists to build a checkpoint at the neck of the
peninsula on which Jamestown sat, so that he
could regulate everyone who came into and left the
settlement.

By the time summer arrived, Jamestown was
doing well, and almost everyone acknowledged that
he had John Smith to thank for his survival through
the winter. Crops were planted, and seventy pigs
were now on Hog Island, and countless chickens
were running around the settlement. Although the
colonists looked forward to the arrival of the next
supply ship from England, they had a growing pride
as they learned how to provide for themselves.

On August 11, 1609, a bell tolled three times,
signifying that a ship was making its way up the
James River. As it turned out, four ships, the
Blessing, the *Falcon,* the *Unity,* and the *Lion,* were
making their way upriver. The four vessels anchored
off Jamestown and several hundred men, women,
and children disembarked. Many of the people were
weak, and some were near death from sunstroke. In
fact, thirty-two passengers had died from the hot
weather on the voyage and had been buried at sea.

Much to John's dismay, John Ratcliffe was aboard one of the ships, as was Gabriel Archer. The two old agitators were back.

John soon learned from Ratcliffe and Archer that the fleet that had set out from England had originally contained nine ships, but one had been forced to turn back early in the voyage, and the four other ships had been separated from the rest in a hurricane in the West Indies. The *Sea Venture,* commanded by Captain Newport, was one of the missing ships, and traveling on board it was Sir Thomas Gates. With great glee Ratcliffe informed John that the board of the Virginia Company of London had decided to greatly increase the size of the colony, hence the large number of new colonists, including entire families. As a result, the board had appointed a governor over the region. The new governor's name was Lord De La Warr, and although he had not yet left England, he had appointed Sir Thomas Gates to act in his stead. The problem was that Sir Thomas was aboard the *Sea Venture,* along with the official orders telling John to step down as president of the colony.

John was shocked and angered by this new turn of events, but he could do little about it as three more ships limped up the James River over the next few days. But the *Sea Venture* did not arrive, and this left John and everyone else in a state of limbo. As he awaited the vessel's arrival, John decided to venture down the James River to look for a suitable site on which to build a fort for some of the new arrivals.

Unlike his other trips, this one made John weary. He had the energy to debate, cajole, and trade with the Indians, but he lacked the patience to try to make the board of the Virginia Company understand how difficult it was to carve a new colony out of the wilderness of North America. For the first time since arriving in Virginia, John wondered whether he should return to England or perhaps stay and help establish one of the smaller colonies he had been informed the Virginia Company intended to establish throughout the area. The decision as to what John should do next, however,was soon taken out of his hands.

Chapter 14

England Again

Boom! A flash of light lit up the darkness. John awoke abruptly from his sleep, with searing pain in his legs and stomach, and then he smelled burning flesh. He leapt up from where he had been sleeping on the deck of the shallop and dived into the water, only to find that the pain prevented him from kicking his legs. He sank beneath the surface and then came up gasping for breath before sinking down again. When he came up a second time, he felt a rescue line that had been thrown overboard, and he grabbed it. The men on the shallop then pulled him back to the boat. As they dragged him up over the side of the vessel, John passed out from the pain. He came to as the men were cutting his charred clothes off him.

John later learned that when one of the men on the shallop had been lighting his tobacco pipe with his tinderbox and flint, a spark had ignited the gunpowder bag hanging from John's waist as he slept. The bag exploded in a ball of flames, burning John, who was now in so much pain that he almost wished that he had drowned in the river. John was barely aware that the colonists on the shallop with him were racing against time to get him back to Jamestown before he died. Fortunately they made it, but little help was to be had at the settlement except for "healing oil" that was so painful to apply that John wondered whether the effort was worth it.

The burns were so severe that John could not walk, and he could barely think straight from the pain. People in the settlement advised him to return to England for treatment, and for once John agreed with them. He knew that he would be useless to the colony for a long time to come.

On October 4, 1609, John was carried aboard the *Unity*. The 570 colonists of Jamestown who gathered to see him leave showed a range of emotions. The twenty or so men who had been with him since the founding of the settlement wept openly, while some of the newcomers seemed glad to be rid of such a strict disciplinarian. John was hardly aware of their presence as he was placed aboard the ship. It was all he could do to prop himself up long enough to see the banks of the James River go by and then the coastline of Chesapeake Bay fade from view. Soon the *Unity* was sailing the open water of the Atlantic Ocean.

John endured the eight-week voyage back to England in great pain, and when the *Unity* docked at Blackwall in London, he was more than happy to disembark, though he still could not walk and had to be helped off the ship. From the dock John hired a sedan chair to take him to a cheap boardinghouse on the Strand, where he set up a new home for himself. It was not much, just a single room with a bed and a chair, but it was all that John needed. John hired a young boy to fetch his meals from a nearby tavern, and he found a doctor who would visit him each morning to dress his burns. It was hardly the homecoming that John deserved, but he was not well enough to contemplate giving speeches and dining with dignitaries. John spent his thirtieth birthday alone in his room, wondering what the future held for him.

Gradually John's burns healed, and his health improved, and John became anxious to know what was going on outside the tiny world he had created for himself at the boardinghouse. One of the captains who had recently sailed to Jamestown visited John upon his return to London. He surprised John by announcing that *A True Relation of Such Occurrences and Accidents of Noate, As Hath Hapned in Virginia Since the First Planting of that Collony,* the manuscript John had sent home from Jamestown with Captain Nelson on the *Phoenix* a year and a half before, had been published and was now a top-selling book in England.

John was astonished by the news, and he contacted the publisher, who informed him that one thousand pounds in royalties was waiting for him to claim. The money helped John get on his feet again, and three months after returning to England, John began to visit some important friends, including Richard Hakluyt. He even met with the members of the board of the Virginia Company and managed to hold his temper as he explained, yet again, how difficult it was to run the colony according to their requirements. John predicted trouble ahead for Jamestown unless the board members stopped obsessing over gold and sent out more able workers and fewer gentlemen as colonists. The members of the board listened respectfully to what John had to say, but a year would pass before the truth of his words would be revealed.

At that time John learned that things had gone badly for the colony almost as soon as he left Jamestown. The new leaders insisted on being treated as superior and took what they wanted from the communal storehouse. And when word was leaked to Chief Powhatan that John was out of the way, the chief saw it as an opportunity to exterminate the Europeans in his territory. He began by killing seventeen of the new colonists who had been sent out to start another settlement farther upriver. By then there were not enough food supplies for the colony to last through the winter, so despite Chief Powhatan's action, John Ratcliffe was forced to try to barter with the chief. John Ratcliffe paid for this effort with his life, as Chief Powhatan was in no mood to help the settlement, and had Ratcliffe killed.

The situation at Jamestown quickly went from bad to worse, until the colonists were forced to resort to eating their cats and dogs, then the rats, and then the leather off their shoes and boots. Finally, in utter desperation, some of the group turned to eating the dead bodies of their fellow colonists. By the time the first supply ship arrived the following spring, only 61 of the 570 colonists John had left behind at Jamestown remained alive.

John was horrified when he heard this. He, more than anyone, could imagine the details of what had happened to the over five hundred people who had perished in what was being called "The Starving Time." Sadly, he concluded that many of the colonists had died needlessly at the hands of incompetent and greedy leaders.

Still, John believed in the future of colonizing Virginia and did what he could to promote it. Buoyed by the success of his first book, he set out to write another, entitled *A Map of Virginia with a Description of the Country*, which was published in 1612. Like John's first book, this new book created a lot of interest, and despite the starving time the previous winter in Jamestown, many more English people wanted to try their luck as colonists in Virginia.

For his part John missed Virginia, but he realized that Lord De La Warr and the council that now ran the colony would not welcome him back. Instead, John's thoughts turned to exploring the coastline north of Chesapeake Bay. The little that was known about this region came from two maps, one dating from his old friend Captain Gosnold's voyage in 1602, and the other from Captain George Weymouth's voyage in 1605. The problem with these two maps was that they contradicted each other at just about every point. John realized that producing an accurate map that showed the coastline, harbors, reefs, inlets, and islands was the first step in colonizing a new area, and he planned to produce that accurate map.

John's main challenge in such an undertaking was finding a sponsor. And then he struck on a simple idea. He knew that the North Atlantic Ocean teemed with whales, cod, and tuna, so why not explore the coastline, trade with the natives, and bring back a haul of salted fish to sell in London? The profit from the sale of the cargo would most likely be enough to finance the entire undertaking. John presented the idea to several investors. The plan made perfect sense to the investors, who advanced the money to buy two ships. By March 1614 John was ready to set sail with the *Frances* and the *Queen Anne,* small square-rigged vessels that were agile in the water and crewed by the best sailors England had to offer. Also aboard the ships were two Indians whom Captain Weymouth had kidnapped and brought back to England nine years before. John made a deal with one of the men, a man named Squanto. If the two Indians would help him navigate along the coast of this region, he would return both men to their homeland before returning to England.

On March 3, 1614, the *Frances* and the *Queen Anne,* carrying a total of forty-five men, sailed out into the English Channel, where they were immediately hit by a raging storm. The vessels were sturdy enough to ride out the storm, however, and they continued their voyage westward. The remainder of the voyage across the Atlantic Ocean was uneventful, and John sighted land off the Grand Banks of Newfoundland in mid-April.

Whales were plentiful in the area, and John decided that the men should try their hand at catching one. But what he thought should have been an easy task turned out to be very difficult. John soon discovered that the great sea mammals were almost impossible to catch, at least given the equipment they had to work with. So John decided to give up his plan to capture whales to take back to England. Instead he concentrated on mapping the coastline and catching tuna and cod to salt and store in the ships' holds.

Before leaving London, John had had seven small boats built, broken down, and lashed to the decks of the *Queen Anne* and the *Frances*. Now that they were off the coast of North America, he had the ships' carpenters put the boats back together so that he and his crew could use them to explore the rivers and inlets along the coast.

The entire venture went just as well as John had expected it would, and in just three months, John was able to chart the coastline of North America south from Nova Scotia and New Brunswick to Rhode Island. He named the area they charted "New England" and gave names to many of the geographic features recorded on the map. These included Cape Cod, which he named after the enormous catch of

cod the men netted in the waters around there, and
Cape Tragabigzanda, which he named after his Turkish mistress when he was a slave in Constantinople.

By mid-July it was time to set out for home. The
holds of both ships were bursting at the seams with
barrels of fish oil, salted fish, and the finest furs
John had traded from the local Indian tribes. As he
had agreed to do, John left Squanto and the other
man with their tribe before setting sail. The voyage
back to London was as pleasant as the journey out
had been, and the sailors spotted the English coastline at the end of August.

Within twenty-four hours of docking in London,
John had sold the entire cargo he had brought back
with him for a profit of eight thousand pounds.
Most of this money had to go to his investors, but
John was able to keep fifteen hundred pounds for
himself. This was enough money for him to live
comfortably on for many years, but John had other
ideas. He wanted to take enough men back to New
England to start his own colony.

This time it was easy to raise money from
investors for the venture, and nine months later
John was ready to set out again for North America.
Under his command were two vessels: one was a
large vessel of two hundred tons, and the other was
a smaller, fifty-ton ship. Together the ships had a
crew of fifty and carried forty-four colonists. John
had handpicked each of the colonists and felt confident that they would form the nucleus of a thriving
community. He planned to lead the colony himself,
and before departing England he told everyone that
he would be away for at least five years.

Fate intervened, however, in the form of a fierce gale 350 miles out to sea. The larger vessel broke her mast and was unable to continue the voyage. With a heavy heart, John ordered the ships back to port. By the time they arrived at Plymouth, the larger ship had taken on so much water that it was beyond repair. While he set about selling the larger vessel for salvage, John had the smaller ship start out again on the voyage to New England, this time by itself. From the money he made selling the stricken ship, John was able to purchase a smaller vessel, and as soon as it was provisioned for the voyage, he set out for New England, hoping to soon catch up to the other ship. Had he known just how perilous the voyage ahead was going to be, John might never have left the dock at Plymouth.

Chapter 15

Pirates

Captain Smith! There's a ship due north of us. I think it's spied us. It's coming about."

John peered through his telescope, and sure enough, a ship was bearing down on them. It was not flying any flags and had four cannons. John immediately suspected that it was a pirate ship.

"All hands on deck. Square the rigging and trim the sails, lads. There's a ship at our tail, and we're going to try to outrun her," John ordered. Right at that moment John wished he had hired an experienced captain for the ship, but being short of money, he had taken on the role himself.

The sailors ran to their stations and did as John had commanded, and soon the sails were billowing as the ship ran before the wind. As the ship raced along, the men strained to adjust the position of the sails so that the sails could catch every puff of wind.

Despite the best effort of the sailors, the pirate ship continued to close the gap on them. Then two jarring cannon shots crossed the bow of John's ship. John knew that the next shot could easily hit the deck and send them to the bottom of the ocean.

"Bring down the sails. We can't outrun her," John yelled as he peered at the looming ship.

The sailors did as John ordered, hauling in the sails and letting the ship drift on the calm sea. As they drifted, the pirate ship sailed right up beside them, and a rough voice with a cockney accent yelled, "Send over the captain. Then we will board you."

John took a deep breath, grabbed a rope that hung from the yardarm above, and swung himself over to the pirate ship. He stood on the deck of the strange vessel, surrounded by men wearing Turkish clothes, complete with silver buckled belts and gem-encrusted swords. Oddly enough, all of the men aboard spoke perfect English.

"We have nothing of value on board," John said as he turned to address the leader of the pirates.

"What is your name?" the leader asked.

"Captain John Smith of London, England," John replied.

"Ah...who would have believed it!" the leader yelled as he gave John a hearty slap on the back. "You don't recognize me, do you? I'll give you a clue. You last saw me, and many of the other men here, I might add, in the Earl of Meldritch's army fighting the Turks beside the Oltu River."

John studied the grinning man in front of him. "Will Fry?" he asked. "It's been over ten years. Is that you?"

Will laughed as he pushed another man in front of John. "Aye, and this is Andy Chambers, your first officer."

John was too stunned to speak, and Will continued on. "After we were marched away, we were sold as slaves to a Turk in Algiers. It has taken us all this time to find a way to escape. But now we have. We have stolen this ship, and now we are masters of our own fates."

As Will spoke, John looked into the weather-beaten faces of the rest of the crew. He recognized several of the men. "What an incredible act of providence!" he exclaimed. "Bring me some wine, and I will tell you why we are on the high seas."

Two hours later John had filled in Will, Andy, and the others on how England was on the brink of establishing colonies up and down the coast of North America. He painted such an optimistic picture of what lay ahead in the New World that the pirates decided to throw their lot in with John and sail their ship on to the American coast with him.

John returned to his ship jubilant. He knew of no men he would rather have under his command than men he had fought with in Hungary against the Turks. Over the next few days on the ship, John heard the story, repeatedly told by the colonists and crew, of how he had saved them from being captured by pirates.

Things were not to be that simple, however. A week later four ships appeared over the horizon.

John judged the largest ship of the four to be over 160 tons. He quickly ordered the British pennant to be raised, and as he glanced over at Will's ship, Will was doing the same thing. But instead of following protocol and hoisting their own colors, the four ships sailed closer and closer and then began peppering the two ships with cannonball shots across their bows. Then they unfurled the gold-and-white lily pennant of France.

John took a deep breath. Since France and England were not at war, he reasoned that this must be a convoy of pirates. Hoping to reason with the commodore of the convoy, John was rowed over to the largest ship, named the *Sauvage*. Negotiations did not go well with Captain d'Elbert, who ordered his crew to man the two English ships while John was to be kept a prisoner on the *Sauvage*. Now six ships were in the pirate convoy, and they set sail southward toward the shipping lanes that Spanish ships used when traveling to and fro between Spain and South America.

Never one to bow to circumstances, John thought up a hundred schemes to escape from the *Sauvage* and flee with his ship. But the fact that he was so well guarded prevented him from acting on these schemes. Instead he decided to try to win the confidence of Captain d'Elbert. To do this, John talked with the captain and helped him plan the capture of three Spanish ships that crossed their bow. Soon Captain d'Elbert was seeking out John every time a new ship appeared over the horizon. John seemed to have an uncanny knack for knowing just the right way to lure a ship into a trap.

One morning John awoke on the *Sauvage* to the yell of a sailor. He soon learned that the crews of the two English ships had thrown their French supervisors overboard and escaped under cover of darkness. John was relieved that his ship was safe, but now he was stuck in the middle of the Atlantic Ocean aboard a French pirate ship.

Now that John had nowhere to escape to, Captain d'Elbert allowed him more freedom. During the next six weeks, the *Sauvage,* accompanied by the other three ships, was able to sink a Scottish ship carrying a load of sugar home from the Caribbean and capture a Portuguese man-of-war laden with gold. Since John had nothing to do aboard the *Sauvage,* between such encounters he asked his captors for a quill pen, ink, and some writing paper. His captors obliged, and John set about writing a manuscript, which he entitled *A Description of New England.* Writing the manuscript renewed John's hope that he would eventually escape the pirate ship and see the rugged coastline of New England once again.

During the capture of the Portuguese man-of-war, Captain d'Elbert had been wounded and soon died of his injury. A new man, Captain Poyrune, took his place, and John set about to win his confidence. This proved to be a difficult job, however, because Captain Poyrune was shrewd and greedy. Still, over the next two weeks John noticed that he was often called to dine with the captain and discuss strategies for capturing ships. Despite John's best advice, Captain Poyrune made enemies of the captains of the other three pirate ships, and one by one the ships slipped away from the convoy.

Then at dinner one night, Captain Poyrune announced to John that they were returning to France. Their destination would be the Île de Ré that lay in the entrance of the bay at the fortress port of La Rochelle on the west coast of France. Situated on this island were go-betweens who would buy a pirate ship's loot with no questions asked and sell it to a merchant for profit. However, returning to France posed one problem: unlike the British, the French government did not tolerate piracy on the high seas, so if the ship was caught before it had stealthily unloaded its cargo on the Île de Ré, everyone aboard would be hanged. Unfortunately, that included John, since he knew that he could not prove that he had been an unwilling participant.

As the ship headed for France, John knew that he had to find a way to get off the vessel at the first opportunity. That opportunity came when the ship ran into a howling November gale as it approached La Rochelle. Because of the storm, Captain Poyrune was forced to take shelter in a small cove at one end of the Île de Ré. Once the ship was safely at anchor in the cove, the entire crew retreated below the rain- and wind-swept deck.

John now had his opportunity. He scooped up the nearly completed manuscript for *A Description of New England,* stuffed it down the front of his shirt, and crept up on deck. With no one around, he was able to lower the smallest of the ship's rowboats into the water and then scramble down a rope into it. Using the small knife he had been allowed to keep with him, he cut the rope, freeing the boat.

John grabbed the oars and began to row as hard as he could. But rowing the small boat in such conditions was no easy job. Waves crashed over the vessel, and John constantly had to stop rowing and bail the boat out to keep it afloat. And while he was bailing, the rowboat drifted with the wind, which was blowing in the opposite direction John wanted to go.

After two hours battling the elements, John had to admit that it did not look like he was going to make it to the safety of the harbor at La Rochelle. The wind had pushed him out to sea, and now the lights of La Rochelle were a faint flicker on the storm-ravaged horizon. But John was not one to accept the inevitable without a fight. He redoubled his effort at the oars, hoping to edge the rowboat closer to shore. But after an hour of doing this, John was finally ready to accept his fate. His boat was being blown farther out into the Atlantic Ocean, where most likely he would die.

As John contemplated this outcome, the wind took a sudden shift in direction. It began blowing the opposite way, pushing the rowboat toward shore. John could scarcely believe it, and he began to row hard again. He passed around the end of the Île de Ré and into the lee of the island where the weather was calmer.

By now John's arms were so tired and sore that he could row no more. In fact, he was so exhausted that he slumped over the oars and fell sound asleep. He was still asleep at the first light of dawn when several customs officers in a longboat intercepted him. Apparently the early-morning incoming tide had steered the rowboat into the harbor at La Rochelle. John had never been so happy in his life to see a boatload of French customs officers.

The customs officers took John to the great hall of the Tower of St. Nicholas, one of the three fortified towers that guarded the entrance to La Rochelle harbor. At the great hall John was fed a hearty breakfast of beef and cheese, which he washed down with several glasses of wine. After breakfast John was taken to see the lord lieutenant of the port and told him the tale of how he had been taken captive by French pirates. The lord lieutenant believed his story and dispatched ships to go and capture the pirate vessel where John said they would find it. But when the vessels got there, it was already too late. The pirate ship had sunk in the storm during the night, and Captain Poyrune and many of his crew had drowned trying to get to shore. As close as he had come to death himself during the night, John recognized that he had probably saved his life by escaping from the ship when he did.

The French authorities did not go away empty-handed, however. They managed to salvage forty thousand pounds worth of goods from the hold of the stricken pirate ship. In the meantime John Smith became the talk of the town. The people of La Rochelle clamored to help him. One woman, who was the widow of a sea captain, gave John all of her late husband's clothes. And so many people wanted to hear about his great adventure that he dined in style each night at people's homes, regaling them with stories.

John stayed in La Rochelle for six weeks before making his way to Paris and then on to Cherbourg, where he found passage on a ship bound for Bristol, England.

By the time John got back to London, word had already gotten around that he was alive and well, and everyone was pleased to see him. But since no one was eager to invest in another scheme to establish a colony in New England, John turned to a familiar way to raise people's interest in the New World. He set to work finishing the manuscript for *A Description of New England.* In the process of completing the manuscript, John learned that the two ships that the French pirates had captured when they took him prisoner had made it safely back to England after their escape. And the smaller ship carrying colonists that he had sent on ahead to New England and had been forced to turn back once again had also made it safely home to England.

On June 3, 1616, John sent the completed manuscript for *A Description of New England* off to the publisher. As coincidence would have it, on that same day Mrs. John Rolfe sailed into Plymouth Harbor in England. Or at least that was her married name. John knew her better as Pocahontas.

Chapter 16

Longing for the New World

John paced the floor as he waited for Pocahontas to enter the parlor in the plush Brentford home where she, her husband, and their entourage were guests. For the first time in a long while, John felt shy. It was seven years and a world away since he had last seen Pocahontas, and he realized that he owed her a great debt. However, it was a debt that he was not in any position to repay, since he lived on a meager income. He felt embarrassed that he could not host Rebecca (the English name Pocahontas now went by), her husband, John, and their baby son in his own home, but the place was barely large enough for him.

Suddenly, as John paced, the door to the parlor opened, and in walked a tall, dark woman, her hair piled on top of her head in an elegant bun. Her silk skirt rustled as she walked toward John. Without warning, she suddenly put her hands over her face and began to sob. Then she turned and abruptly left the room. John did not know what to do, so he waited.

Soon a man entered the parlor and introduced himself as John Rolfe. "I am sorry," he said, "but Rebecca had been told you were dead, so she was a little overcome to actually see you in person."

"That I can see," John replied.

"I am sure she will be fine soon. In the meantime let us have a glass of wine. I've heard a lot about you, Captain Smith, and should like to be better acquainted with you," John Rolfe said.

Over the next two hours, John Smith recounted much of the early history of Jamestown. He told about how they selected the site for the settlement, about clearing the land and building cottages for the men to live in, and about their early dealings and skirmishes with the Indians.

In return John Rolfe answered questions about how the colony was doing now. He also told John that he believed that the future of Jamestown lay in gold—not the kind of gold that comes from mines but the gold-leaf tobacco plant. In fact, John Rolfe had brought this particular variety of tobacco plant up from the West Indies, and the plant had adapted remarkably well to the climate of Virginia, so much so that although he had exported four barrels of the leaves in March 1614, he had brought back 2,300 pounds of tobacco leaves to sell while he was home. And he hoped to send 50,000 pounds of tobacco leaf back to England by 1620. John Smith was most impressed.

When Rebecca entered the room again two hours later, she apologized for her behavior. "It was a shock," she told John. "Those at Jamestown said you were dead, but I did not know for sure, because your countrymen lie a lot. My father Powhatan commanded Tomocomo to seek you and find out the truth."

"You have Tomocomo with you?" John asked, glad to have a neutral topic to talk about.

"Yes, my father sent him along on the voyage, though Tomocomo is not enjoying himself nearly as much as I am. He disdains the Christian religion, which I have embraced, and he scoffs at accompanying me to balls and plays. I think he is eager to return to our home."

"And what about you? Do you want to go back?" John asked.

Rebecca shook her head. "Some things about this place do not agree with me. The smoke here is different, not the white smoke of a wood-stoked fire but the black, billowing smoke from many coal fires. It lodges in my chest and makes me cough. But this is my New World, and I am enjoying exploring it."

John smiled. "I see we are both explorers at heart!" he laughed.

Later that night, as John left the house, he was struck by the incredible situation he had just found himself in. He was alive because Pocahontas had risked her life to save his, and she was in England because he had welcomed her as a visitor in Jamestown and taught her how to speak English.

He hoped their next reunion would be in Jamestown, but it was not to be. In March 1617, the Rolfe family embarked on the return voyage to Virginia. They were still sailing down the Thames River when Rebecca became ill with pneumonia. Her lungs had been so weakened by the damp English weather and the polluted air of London that her condition quickly deteriorated. The captain ordered the ship to land, and she was taken ashore. But that night, Rebecca Rolfe (Pocahontas) died, leaving behind a baby son and a distraught husband.

The following year John learned that Poca-hontas's father, Chief Powhatan, had also died and that the chief's younger brother Opechancanough had succeeded him as the great chief of the Powhatan confederation of tribes.

The next year more news filtered back to John from the colony. In the fall of 1619 a group of Dutch privateers anchored off Jamestown in their ship the *White Lion.* Aboard the ship were twenty black African slaves, who had been on board a Portuguese slave ship bound for Vera Cruz, Mexico, when the privateers overran the vessel. The captain of the *White Lion,* John Jope, traded the ten men and ten women for corn to provision his ship. The Africans were immediately put to work harvesting the tobacco crop, a backbreaking, labor-intensive job. The slaves were the first colonists who had not settled willingly in the British New World.

At the same time another group of would-be colonists crossed John's path. Calling themselves Separatists, they were a group of Christians who criticized the Church of England for not following the Bible closely enough. The group had created so much controversy in England that about one hundred of them eventually fled to Holland, where they set up a community. However, over the course of the ten years they had been there, they realized that living in Holland was not the answer to their problems. Their children were growing up speaking Dutch and were leaning toward Dutch traditions instead of the Separatist ways. After reading John Smith's books on Virginia and studying the maps John had drawn, the Separatists had set their sights on establishing their own colony in the New World.

The Separatists were so serious about their plan that William Brewster, their leader in Holland, returned to England to hold secret talks with John. William risked his life in doing so, because King James wanted him hanged for treason. At the secret talks William offered John the job of military protector of the new colony the Separatists planned to set up, but John turned down the offer. He could see that William was just as stubborn as he was, and he knew that the two of them would eventually disagree strongly on religious issues and on how to run the colony.

Still, John watched with interest as the near penniless group of Separatists organized themselves. The group managed to obtain permission to set up a colony at the mouth of the Hudson River, and 102 colonists, about half of them Separatists, packed themselves onto a chartered ship, the *Mayflower,* for the voyage across the Atlantic Ocean to the New World. In the New World they would soon band together as one group known as the Pilgrims.

The first report back from the Pilgrims told how they had made a mistake in navigation on the journey. Instead of reaching land at the mouth of the Hudson River, they had eventually arrived at a place farther north. On his exploration of the coast of New England, John had named the place where they landed New Plymouth. Weary and confused, the Pilgrims chose to stay there and set up a colony rather than press on to their original destination. As with the founders of Jamestown thirteen years before, the Pilgrims were plagued with illness and hunger, and fewer than half of the members of the colony survived the first winter.

In contrast, by 1620 Jamestown had turned into a thriving settlement and the hub of an ever-expanding network of tobacco plantations. Over twelve hundred colonists now lived in and around Jamestown, and John hoped that more colonists would set out for the colony. To help give emigration to Virginia a boost, in 1621 John began to write another book, entitled *The Generall Historie of Virginia, New England and the Summer Isles* [Bermuda]. Bermuda had become an important stopping-off point for English ships coming and going to North America.

John was partway through writing the book when the *Sea Flower* sailed into port at Bristol, bearing horrifying news. Four months before, on Friday, March 22, 1622, Chief Opechancanough had led surprise attacks on most of the plantations and settlements around Jamestown. Letters home to the Virginia Company from survivors described the gruesome way in which about 350 colonists had been killed.

With over a quarter of the population of Jamestown dead and the rest living in fear for their lives, the governor of the colony closed most of the plantations and ordered everyone back to the settlement, which was fortified further against Indian attack.

John was appalled and angered when he heard the news. He was appalled because of the great loss of life, and especially the death of his old friend Nathaniel Powell, who had accompanied him on the voyage up the James River in 1607. And he was angry because he believed that the members of the Virginia Company had not taken the time to understand the way the Indians thought, and as a result they had let down their guard and provided opportunity for the Indians to strike. The leaders of Jamestown had given up on holding regular military maneuvers and living in fortified settlements in favor of establishing plantations and planting tobacco. No wonder, John thought, that the Indians saw the opportunity to attack such a weak and trusting people.

As a result of the massacre, the board of the Virginia Company was determined not to be taken advantage of again by the Indians. They chose to meet violence with violence and circulated a tract outlining their plan of action. John read the tract in disbelief.

Because our hands which before were tied with gentlenesse and faire usage, are now set at liberty by the treacherous violence of the savages, not untying the knot, but cutting it: So that we, who hitherto have had possession of no more ground than their waste [that is, they used only their "spare" land], and our purchase at a valuable consideration to their owne contentment, gained; may now by right of warre, and the law of nations, invade the country, and destroy them who sought to destroy us: whereby wee shall enjoy their cultivated places, turning the laborious mattocke [hoe] into the victorious sword.

It seemed to John that all hope of the Indians and colonists living peacefully together was over. Virginia was now a colony at war with the natives. John wrote to the board of the Virginia Company with a different solution. He urged the company to send him and one hundred soldiers under his command to Virginia, where he would protect the settlers and negotiate with the Indians. He felt sure that he could find a way to stop the killing.

The reply he received back was as insulting to John as it was disturbing. The members of the board of the Virginia Company said that they did not have the money to support one hundred soldiers, and they suggested that John raise the army himself and pay their costs. In return, John and his company of soldiers would be free to kill as many Indians as they liked and to keep half of whatever they could plunder from them.

John despaired and fumed. Had the members of the board learned nothing from all of his letters and pleadings to them? The natives of Virginia did not have anything of value except for their corn stores. They had no gold pots, no sapphire necklaces, no silver chest plates.

One year later, five hundred more colonists had died at Jamestown, some from disease and illness, but most at the hands of the Indians. Instead of leading another coordinated massacre, warriors had picked off the colonists by ones or twos as they went about their gardening or hunted in the forest for food.

John felt vindicated when King James decided to carry out an investigation into the workings of the Virginia Company. The court of inquiry into the matter found that the Virginia Company had not done enough to protect the colonists under its care. As a result, King James revoked the company's royal charter. Jamestown and Virginia were now the property of the king of England, not a group of investors.

Besides making John feel that he had been proven right, the takeover of Virginia by King James had another positive effect. Late in 1622 John completed the manuscript for *The Generall Historie of Virginia, New England and the Summer Isles,* which was subsequently published. All of the controversy over Virginia created an instant market for the book, the sales of which were strong from the beginning.

A year after its completion, the book needed updating. The Dutch West India Company had established a colony of its own in the New World. The colony was called New Amsterdam and was situated on the island of Manhattan at the mouth of the Hudson River, where the Pilgrims had originally been planning to establish their colony. The Dutch colony was founded on the principles of religious freedom and open trade and was protected by professional soldiers. John admired the sensible way the Dutch were going about setting up their colony.

Farther north the tiny French fort of Quebec was also growing. In fact, its population had reached eighty people, and the French government was actively promoting the colony, called New France, as a crossroads for fur trappers, explorers, and missionaries.

John continued to write, and in 1626 *An Accidence* [Primer], *or the Pathway to Experience* was published. It was a practical, step-by-step guide to sailing and fighting at sea and became an instant classic.

By now John was forty-six years old, an old man by the standards of the time, and he had given up hope of returning to the New World. Instead, he contented himself with knowing that he had played a vital part in the beginnings of the English colonies there, and he continued that legacy through his writing.

In 1630 John published *The True Travels, Adventures, and Observations of Captaine John Smith.* This book dealt mainly with John's early experiences in Western and Central Europe. It helped to answer the public's questions about John's early life. As he wrote the book, even John was astonished by some of the bizarre situations he had managed to get himself into during those years.

After the publication of this book, John set out to write *Advertisements* [Information] *for the Unexperi-*

enced Planters of New England or Any Where. The book was published in May 1631, just as John's health began to fail. John's legs swelled up so much that he could not walk, and he coughed incessantly. Fearing that the end of his life was near, he called for a lawyer and dictated a will. But he was too weak to sign his name at the end of the document.

John Smith died ten days later on June 21, 1631, at the age of 51. On the nightstand beside his bed lay a copy of his book *A Description of New England.* In the book John had argued that English Americans had a unique opportunity to create their own destiny, unlike workers in England who were bound by a rigid class system. John wrote,

> Here [in New England] every man may be master and owner of his owne labour and land; or the greatest part in a small time. If hee have nothing but his hands, he may set up this trade; and by industrie quickly grow rich;... If he have but the taste of virtue, and magnanimitie [ambition], what to such a minde can be more pleasant, than planting and building a foundation for his posteritie, gotte from the rude earth, by God's blessing and his owne industrie, without prejudice to any.

This was Captain John Smith's vision for the Royal British Colonies of North America. John had spent much of his life helping to establish a foothold in the New World for these colonies. Only time would tell how well future generations would build on that foothold.

Bibliography

arbour, Philip L. *The Three Worlds of Captain John Smith*. Boston: Houghton Mifflin, 1964.

Bridenbaugh, Carl. *Jamestown 1544–1699*. New York: Oxford University Press, 1980.

Fishwick, Marshall W. *Jamestown: First English Colony*. New York: American Heritage, 1965.

Gerson, Noel B. *Survival: Jamestown: First English Colony in America*. New York: Julian Messner, 1967.

Lewis, Paul. *The Great Rogue: A Biography of Captain John Smith*. New York: David McKay Company, 1966.

Price, David A. *Love and Hate in Jamestown: John Smith, Pocahontas, and the Heart of a New Nation*. New York: Alfred A. Knopf, 2003.

Syme, Ronald. *John Smith of Virginia*. New York: William Morrow & Company, 1954.

About the Authors

Janet and Geoff Benge are a husband and wife writing team with more than thirty years of writing experience. Janet is a former elementary school teacher. Geoff holds a degree in history. Originally from New Zealand, the Benges spent ten years serving with Youth With A Mission. They have two daughters, Laura and Shannon, and an adopted son, Lito. They make their home in the Orlando, Florida, area.